trotman

D1584228

Performing Arts

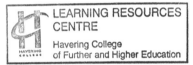
UNCOVERED

Performing Arts Uncovered
This first edition published in 2004 by Trotman and Company Ltd
2 The Green, Richmond, Surrey TW9 1PL

Editorial and Publishing Team
Author Dee Pilgrim
Editorial Mina Patria, Editorial Director; Rachel Lockhart,
Commissioning Editor; Anya Wilson, Editor;
Bianca Knights, Assistant Editor
Production Ken Ruskin, Head of Pre-press and Production
Sales and Marketing Deborah Jones, Head of Sales and Marketing
Advertising Tom Lee, Commercial Director
Managing Director Toby Trotman

British Library Cataloguing in Publication Data
A catalogue record for this book is available
from the British Library

ISBN 1 84455 002 8

Typeset by Palimpsest Book Production Limited,
Polmont, Stirlingshire

Printed and bound in Great Britain by Cromwell Press,
Trowbridge, Wiltshire

CONTENTS

ACKNOWLEDGEMENTS   V

ABOUT THE AUTHOR   VI

INTRODUCTION
WHAT'S THE STORY, MORNING
GLORY?   1

CHAPTER 1
LIGHTS, CAMERA, ACTION!   9

CHAPTER 2
A LIFE LESS ORDINARY   13

CHAPTER 3
DRAMA QUEENS (AND KINGS)   22

CHAPTER 4
COURSES FOR HORSES   31

CHAPTER 5
LET'S FACE THE MUSIC   45

CHAPTER 6
SINGING FOR YOUR SUPPER   70

CHAPTER 7
I COULD HAVE DANCED
ALL NIGHT   79

CHAPTER 8
DANCING QUEENS
(AND KINGS)   88

CHAPTER 9
A WORLD IN MOTION   96

CHAPTER 10
OPPORTUNITY KNOCKS   104

CHAPTER 11
THE FINAL WORD   108

RESOURCES   110

Acknowledgements

Many thanks to the people who agreed to be interviewed for this book and for the many useful insights they gave me into the performing arts as a profession. I would especially like to thank Tania Peach for arranging for me to visit Mountview Academy and would also like to thank the members of the Critics' Circle who offered extremely useful contacts. Ian Bramley at Dance UK and Harriet Wigginton at the Council for Dance Education and Training (CDET) were both extremely helpful, as was Nicole Hay of The National Council for Drama Training (NCDT) who provided me with course information. Kelly Wiffen at Equity provided the figures for Equity minimum wage rates. I would also like to thank the National Music Council (NMC) for the use of facts and figures from its 2002 'Counting The Notes' report. Many thanks to The Society of London Theatre for the use of information from its 1999 'After Wyndham (key issues in London Theatre)' report (written by Tony Travers of LSE). Finally, a huge thank-you to Carlton Edwards, my songwriting partner in crime.

About the Author

Dee Pilgrim completed the pre-entry, periodical journalism course at the London College of Printing before working on a variety of music and women's titles. As a freelancer and full-time member of staff she has written numerous articles and interviews for *Company, Cosmopolitan, New Woman, Woman's Journal* and *Weight Watchers* magazines. For many years she covered new output by singer/songwriters for *Top* magazine, which was distributed via Tower record stores, and during this period interviewed the likes of Tori Amos, Tom Robinson, and Joan Armatrading. As a freelancer for Independent Magazines she concentrated on celebrity interviews and film, theatre and restaurant reviews for such titles as *Ms London, Girl About Town, LAM* and *Nine To Five* magazines, and in her capacity as a critic she has appeared on both radio and television. She is currently the Film Reviewer for *Now* magazine. When not attending film screenings she is active within the Critics' Circle and is on the committee for their annual film awards event. Dee is a published songwriter and is currently engaged in writing the narrative to an as yet unpublished trilogy of children's illustrated books.

What's the Story, Morning Glory?

So, you want to be in pictures? You want to make it big on *Fame Academy*, or maybe even dance all night? You want to smell the greasepaint and stand in the spotlights while an adoring audience hangs on your every word? Well, then you'll be joining a very large club because these days everybody seems to want to be a performer.

It's really no surprise the performing arts are such a popular career choice because for those actors, musicians and dancers who do last in the business the rewards – both personal and financial – can be huge. There are the critically acclaimed films, albums and dance pieces, a public that loves you, a large salary, and the glamorous lifestyle celebrity can bring. But there is also the downside, the constant pressure of being in the public eye, the uncertainty if it will all last, then the times when you have a flop, when your agent stops ringing, and the public doesn't seem to love you any more. And this is what you have to look forward to if you actually make it – the sad fact is that most never even get that far.

THE FAME GAME

Andy Warhol once said that everybody 'will be famous for fifteen minutes'. For some fifteen minutes is all they ever get, for others it is more like fifteen seconds. For every actress that wins an award there are a thousand still waiting tables, temping in offices, and longing for their big break. For every White Stripes there are a dozen would-be bands sitting in dingy rehearsal studios waiting to be discovered, and for every ballerina like Darcey Bussell there is a flock of dying swans. This is a tough business, a profession that takes no prisoners, a career where you are ultimately your own product and must keep selling yourself each and every day. This is no place for shrinking violets.

GETTING IN THE KNOW

But if you've picked up this book it means you are interested in learning more about the performing arts. You want the real story on what it's all about, what you should expect, and what you can actually do in the business. You want to know what makes performing such a pleasure and joy, but also what makes it such a pain. You want to find out what people in the industry already have experienced, how and where they trained, and where their careers are going. Finally, you want to know what qualifications you will need to pursue your dream of becoming an actor or actress, musician or dancer. *Performing Arts Uncovered* is an honest appraisal of the industry, and what you can realistically achieve within it. It has to be because there is no use coming into this business with false illusions; there are already too many failed performers out there.

'You need to have a sense of humour and you need flexibility, humility and determination to make it in this industry.'

Kate Gielgud, actress/voice coach

THE RIGHT DIRECTION

For the purposes of this book we will be looking at the three main sections of the performing arts: drama, music, and dance. You will find the main body of the book itself has been split into these three categories for ease of use. Deciding where jobs in the performing arts actually begin and end is a bit like asking how long is a piece of string. Basically, the string goes on as long as you are prepared to unravel it. This is because the industry is so very vast, generating billions of pounds in revenue and employing thousands of people in hundreds of different positions (everything from ticket-office staff to international stars). Instead of trying to cover every job, this book concentrates on those individuals closest to the performance process itself, i.e. the actors, musicians, and dancers, although other, related jobs are also included and their roles explained. This means if you decide that performing is not for you, you may well find mentioned here some other position within the industry that suits you better.

THE SHOW MUST GO ON

The advent of new technology – increasing satellite and cable channels, DVD, Mini Disc, the iPod and mobile telephone wizardry – means the whole world now really *is* a stage and that in turn means we need more performers than ever before out there strutting their stuff. This book will help you decide whether you could be one of them. In the theatre they say 'break a leg' when they want to wish an actor luck. However, luck is a difficult commodity to come by. Much better to read this book, know the low-down, be prepared and go into the industry with your eyes wide open, then the luck takes care of itself.

'When you're an actor, there's nothing better than working with other actors, rather than sitting at home alone waiting for the phone to ring.'
                    Kate Gielgud, actress/voice coach

FASCINATING FACT

Worldwide earnings of the biggest British theatre shows dwarf those of Hollywood blockbuster films such as *Titanic*.
                    Source: *The Wyndham Report*

JARGON BUSTERS
CHAIR
In theatre, each different musician has a different 'chair' within the musicians' 'pit' (see below). So, if there are three keyboard players, their three different chairs are called Keyboards 1, Keyboards 2 and Keyboards 3. In London's West End once you have a specific chair then the chair is yours for life unless you do something terribly wrong. 'For life' can mean as long as the show lasts or for as long as you want the job. Some musicians have had their chairs on *Les Miserables* since it opened over 18 years ago.

CORPSING
When an actor or actress cannot keep a straight face and bursts into fits of giggles mid-performance they are said to have 'corpsed'. Nicholas Lyndhurst who plays Rodney in *Only Fools And Horses* is a serial corpser, as anyone who has seen his out-takes on *It'll Be Alright On The Night* will know.

DIGS
The affectionate term for the boarding houses, bed and breakfast or other cheap, rented accommodation actors still use while on tour. Spotlight's excellent *Contacts* book contains a Good Digs Guide (see Resources).

DRYING
'Drying' is when an actress or actor forgets their lines mid-performance (as in they have 'dried up'). If they do so on stage you may hear them say 'prompt' (see below).

FRONT OF HOUSE
At one time, theatres were known as 'playhouses', which is why to this day backstage staff may ask if such-and-such an actor is 'in the house' (i.e. is he actually on the premises). Front of house refers to exactly that, the part of the theatre that is in front of the stage and backstage areas and includes the box office, foyers, bars and auditorium. Front of house staff include ticket sellers, ushers, theatre managers and bar staff.

GIG

Although the word gig is normally associated with the music world, actors use it as well. It basically means a job, so Coldplay may talk about doing a 'gig' at Brixton Academy, while to an actor a 'gig' may be work on an advert or a stint on tour.

THE PIT

The orchestra pit in a theatre. At classical concerts the orchestra is normally on stage in open view of the audience, but in ballet performances and in musical theatre the musicians are usually hidden from view in the pit.

PROMPT

The prompter, or better known as the prompt, sits out of sight of the audience in a theatre reading the written play or script as the actors perform it. If an actor forgets their lines, the prompt will then assist them by reading out the next few words of the script in order to jog their memory.

REPERTORY COMPANY

A theatre group that specialises in limited runs of a series of plays or pieces they have in their repertoire (hence the name) rather than on long runs of the same play. The repertory company is now something of a rarity.

RESTING

The polite term used when actors are out of work.

THE RIDER

A term dear to the hearts of rock bands everywhere. The rider is the provisions the concert promoter agrees to leave for the band in the backstage area. This will mostly consist of both soft and alcoholic drinks as well as some form of food. Certain major stars are so fussy about their rider they get very upset if it does not tally with what is stipulated in their contract. One very well-known star is rumoured to have had a major tantrum when she discovered her rider contained the wrong-coloured jelly babies!

ROADIES

The real term for roadies is road crew. They are an important part of any live tour, be it theatrical, dance or music. They are responsible for taking down all the stage rigging, including mikes, lighting, special effects and amplifiers, packing them up and then transporting them (quite often right through the night and across country borders) on to the next venue on the tour. For a rock band such as Pink Floyd, renowned for its spectacular live shows, the road crew can employ substantial amounts of people. At present roadies are not unionised but an initiative is being started in summer 2004 by the GMB union, Britain's general trade union, to explain the benefits union membership can bring (including access to pension plans and legal advice).

SHOWREEL

A showreel is like an audio/visual CV. Actors, dancers and musicians will edit down highlights of their performances onto a video and present this during casting calls or at auditions. It gives the casting agent or show's director and producer an indication of what each candidate is capable of. Showreels should look professional and so can be expensive to produce but remember: you are your own product and you deserve to get the best marketing money can buy.

TECHIES

The affectionate term for technical staff or technicians. The techies handle all the technical stuff such as lighting, rigging, sound, scenery, special effects, etc. Without them most modern-day theatrical performances, concerts, TV shows and films could not be produced.

'If you are coming into this industry because you "want to be famous", then, in my opinion, you are likely to be disappointed at some stage along the line, even if you succeed.'

Jonathan Goodwin, professional magician, five tv's *Monkey Magic*

FASCINATING FACT

The Universal Music Group is the biggest music group in the world. Its artists include Eminem, Daniel Beddingfield and Jamie Cullum.

A NICE DAY AT THE OFFICE

Unless you are working in a secretarial or administration position within the performing arts you probably won't be located in an office. It's far more likely you will be in a rehearsal room, on stage in a theatre or concert hall, on a sound stage at a film or TV studio, in a recording studio, or on location. What you do at all these different places will depend on whether you are involved in drama, music or dance. See the chart below for just some of the different sites you could be working at in the performing arts – and some of the many different projects you could be working on.

JOBS IN PERFORMING ARTS

Lights, Camera, Action!

DRAMA UNCOVERED

Once upon a time actors knew their place; it was on the stage where they plied their trade. These days they are everywhere; the proliferation of new media means the world of acting impinges on our real-life world on a day-to-day basis. Turn on your radio and there's *The Archers*, the long-running tale of life down on the farm and in the village of Ambridge. Radio is the medium where many new writers get their first break. For example, *Little Britain* was a radio programme before it hit our TV screens.

WHERE DO ACTORS WORK?

On TV, actors pop up in soaps, serious dramas, light comedies and you can't even avoid them during the ad breaks – chances are that the person extolling the virtues of a certain brand of toilet paper is an actor, too. At least if you go to the cinema or theatre you are making a positive choice to see actors at work, but what about at a corporate event, a murder-mystery weekend break or even at a children's party? If you decide to watch a dedicated music channel like MTV actors even turn up in the videos – you simply can't avoid them, especially in a world where new satellite and cable channels are hungry for drama programmes to fill their schedules. There has even been an interactive 'film' on the web called *Running Time* where viewers could watch a five-minute episode and then choose one of three options as to what would happen to the actors in the next instalment.

WHAT OPPORTUNITIES ARE THERE?

You don't necessarily have to have had formal training to become an actor – temperament and character have as much to do with working in the industry as any qualifications you may or may not have. However, these days it really does help to have some sort of training as well as experience. This is because it will give you the skills to succeed and mark you out as a professional. Once you have completed an accredited course you will be eligible for full membership of the British actors' union, Equity, which means you will have a much better chance of getting professional jobs. According to the 2002 Census, 21,132 people stated they were actors working as employees while 17,697 were self-employed (Equity has approximately 36,000 members, but this includes dancers and other performers as well). That's a lot of people acting up and down the country. The story doesn't end there either. Behind every actor is a small army of people who are just as essential for getting a production – be it on stage, radio or screen – ready and rolling. There are the writers, directors and producers, the voice coaches, costume designers and managers. Most importantly, there is the backstage staff such as the lighting and sound technicians, the riggers and prop buyers. Then there are the people you might not even think about but who still have their part to play, such as ticket sales agents, theatre and cinema managers and ushers, theatrical agents and even film company lawyers.

In this book we will be concentrating most on actual performers and those people who have the roles closest to them. Take a look at the 'Jobs in Drama' chart. Although it is not totally comprehensive, it will give you some indication of the vast wealth of careers you could pursue in the acting branch of the performing arts profession.

FASCINATING FACT

Drama is the 8th most popular degree to take at university after Business Management, Computer Science, Law, Design Studies, Psychology, English Literature and Medicine. UCAS had 39,398 applications to Drama courses in 2001.

Source: UCAS

JOBS IN DRAMA

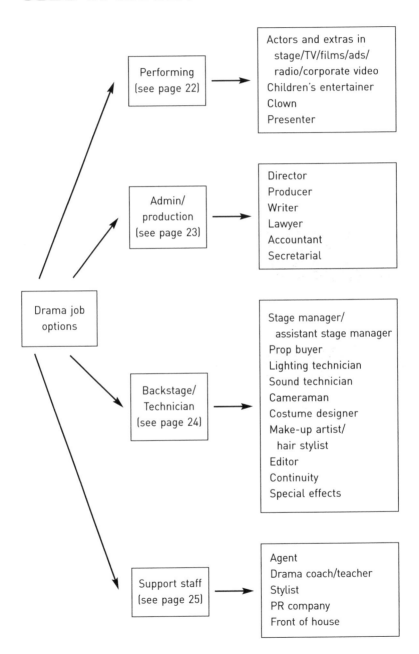

Drama job options

Performing
(see page 22)

Actors and extras in
   stage/TV/films/ads/
   radio/corporate video
Children's entertainer
Clown
Presenter

Admin/
production
(see page 23)

Director
Producer
Writer
Lawyer
Accountant
Secretarial

Backstage/
Technician
(see page 24)

Stage manager/
   assistant stage manager
Prop buyer
Lighting technician
Sound technician
Cameraman
Costume designer
Make-up artist/
   hair stylist
Editor
Continuity
Special effects

Support staff
(see page 25)

Agent
Drama coach/teacher
Stylist
PR company
Front of house

SPOTLIGHT ON SPOTLIGHT

Spotlight was founded in 1927 to provide casting information to the entertainment industry. For over 75 years portraits and profiles of actors and actresses have appeared in Spotlight and casting directors have searched this unique database to find the perfect artist for the part. Getting into Spotlight will enhance your profile considerably – in fact, some actors consider it essential.

- Spotlight now has over 30,000 artists on its books

- The Spotlight interactive website receives over 10 million page impressions a year

- Every month, over 10,000 artists are put forward for over 700 roles via the Spotlight link

- Spotlight publishes the invaluable annual *Contacts* book that lists everything from agents to film and television distributors, opera companies to set construction.

Source: Spotlight: www.spotlightcd.com
(For more information see Resources.)

A Life Less Ordinary

If your idea of the ideal job is a well-paid, nice, secure 9 to 5 with at least four weeks' paid holiday a year, then you can rule out being an actor straightaway. The biggest downsides of this profession, as any actor worth her salt will tell you, are:

INSECURITY

According to Equity, the actors' and performers' trade union (see Resources), which has roughly 36,000 members, an average member may only work 12.4 weeks of the year. Obviously, if you are in a long-running TV series or theatre production, you will be guaranteed more work than this, but at any one time it is estimated only a quarter of actors in this country are actually working. This means for many jobbing actors performing is a hand-to-mouth existence where they must constantly hustle for work, send off their CVs, attend auditions and keep up with contacts. This can cause financial insecurity (see below). Even worse, constant rejection, when you keep going up for jobs and not getting them, can cause distressing emotional insecurity, which in turn can affect an actor's performance. The way most actors deal with this is by having an alternative day job, and by keeping busy doing other things.

'When people are not ringing you up it really chips away at your self-esteem, so you need to go off and do other things like unpaid read-throughs of new plays, workshops, and voice work.'

Kate Gielgud, actress/voice coach

LOW PAY

If you think all actors live in flash houses and drive expensive cars, think again. Of course, the big stars are well recompensed for their work, but most actors only earn modest wages throughout their careers. While people like Billy Connolly may have now joined the $1 million-a-film club (he was rumoured to earn this for his appearance in *The Last Samurai*), Equity members can earn as little as £300 a week. This is why it is so important to have another skill that can earn you money while you are 'resting', such as secretarial or IT skills. We will explore the financial aspects of acting more in Chapter 3.

ANTISOCIAL HOURS

If you like going out in the evenings and having weekends free to spend with friends then live theatre work really won't suit you. Your weekday evenings will be spent performing and most Saturdays will consist of two performances (the matinee and evening performances). Even if you become a regular on a TV soap the hours will be very long because you have to cram in so much filming every day. This is especially true during the shooting of a film where your make-up call can come at 4am, while the last scene of the day may not be shot until after 10pm. The schedule becomes even more frantic if you are shooting on location and have to wait for bad weather to pass. (If you want to see just how bad shooting on location can get watch a copy of *Lost In La Mancha*, the documentary of director Terry Gilliam's disastrous attempts to film *Don Quixote* with Johnny Depp on location in Spain.)

FASCINATING FACT

Incoming big-budget films such as *Troy, Alexander*, and *Harry Potter* helped push UK production to £1.17bn in 2003, a record high. Indigenous films (i.e. productions

instigated here) such as *Bride And Prejudice* and *Ladies In Lavender* spent £277.7 million, and prospects remain strong for 2004.

Source: *Screen International* magazine

ACTING UP

If there are so many downsides to this profession, why do people want to do it in the first place? The answer is simple: people become actors and actresses because they *love* performing. It gives them a legitimate excuse to play to an audience, and to be the centre of attention. For most it is a vocation, not a calculated career move. Some are more suited to the profession than others, which will mainly come down to natural-born talent, however, there are other personal and physical factors that will help you be a success in the acting world.

STAMINA

Acting is not for the faint of heart or the weak of body. The hours are long, the work can be physically demanding and the pressures – and most especially the performances – can be emotionally draining. You have to look after yourself. This is especially true of young women in the profession who sometimes feel under pressure to be very thin and to watch their diet. Many actors now take courses such as yoga, Pilates and meditation to ensure they keep their bodies and minds in tip-top shape.

ABILITY TO WORK IN A TEAM

Unless you are putting on a one-man play by yourself, most theatrical, TV or film performances are collaborative efforts. There may be a great many other actors performing with you, then there's the director, maybe the writer, the stage manager and all the backstage staff to consider. You will have to interact with all these other people and so being a team player is essential. In fact, one aspect of the profession many people love is the great feeling of camaraderie that can build up between members of a cast and its crew, and the friendships that are made and can last a lifetime.

COMMUNICATION SKILLS

Think about what an actor actually does. He or she is conveying words and concepts written by a playwright or scriptwriter to an audience. You really do have to have a way with words and with physical gestures in order to make the message clear. You also need to understand directions given to you and to be able to make yourself understood. This is why a confident and clear voice is essential.

FLEXIBILITY

As you will have seen by now, an actor's life is anything other than ordinary. One week you could be doing a comedy cameo in panto in Blackpool, the next month doing a voiceover for a TV advert in London, and the month after that you could be playing a serious role on tour in Europe. If you can adapt to a career that is constantly changing and see it as an exciting challenge then acting could be for you.

TRANSFERABLE SKILLS

You'll also need to be flexible when 'resting'. If you read the case studies dotted throughout this book you will see that time and time again actors, dancers and musicians talk about the need to have other skills outside of their 'proper' job so they can earn money while not working. These jobs need to be short term or freelance so if a gig does come up suddenly you have the flexibility to be able to take it. For actors, ideal jobs include waiting tables, working as bar staff, telesales, office work, teaching acting classes, or getting training to be a practitioner such as voice coach, masseuse, or yoga, t'ai chi or Pilates instructor. Remember: in this profession you are guaranteed to have periods of unemployment, so you need to have another string to your bow so you can weather the financial bad times.

GOOD MEMORY

Actors have to memorise lines, it is a big part of their jobs, and often they will have a very short period in order to learn their parts (this is especially true on TV soap operas where shooting is very fast). Because of this having a good memory is essential and it can also help where contacts are concerned. People tend to move around within the industry a lot and remembering their names, faces and where you know them from will stand you in good stead at auditions and open calls.

APPEARANCE

All the actors interviewed for this book agreed on one thing: an attractive appearance is one of your biggest assets in the modern industry. Nine times out of ten, if two equally talented actors go up for a job, the most attractive of the pair will get it. Actors such as Mackenzie Crook (*The Office*, *Pirates of the Caribbean*) have shown this is not always the case, and have made an asset out of having a face with strong character, but you should be aware that you might sometimes lose out on a job because of the way you look.

DETERMINATION

Whatever else you do in this industry, the one thing you can never do is give up. Keep on smiling, even when you haven't had a job for months, and keep sending out those CVs and going to those auditions. You have to be tenacious and optimistic because the only person who can really sell your talents is you. No actor ever made it by sitting in a corner lamenting their fate. Get out there, be seen, and shine!

ADD-ONS

One of the best ways to increase your worth as an actor or actress is to have add-on skills. These are the extra skills you can learn that may come in useful one day, the most basic being having a clean driving licence (you never know, you might end up on a TV series driving an ambulance), while the more exotic include fire eating, horse riding, ability to play the piano and to swordfight. Many of the better drama schools teach certain add-ons as a matter of course, but it's never too late to learn a few off your own bat as well.

DON'T PUT YOUR DAUGHTER ON THE STAGE, MRS WORTHINGTON!

'Her personality
Is not in reality
Inviting enough,
Exciting enough
For this particular sphere.'

So wrote Noel Coward. Even if you have great natural talent as an actor, there are some personality traits and physical conditions that can hold you back. You may not suffer from any of them now, but it is good to know what they are, and to monitor yourself for them in the future.

READING DIFFICULTIES/DYSLEXIA

As we've already seen, learning lines is a big part of any actor's job. Therefore, if you find reading difficult, or suffer from dyslexia, this may not be the profession for you and you may find a backstage or support staff role better utilises other skills and talents you have.

CHRONIC SHYNESS

Isn't it funny how some of us can be veritable Nicole Kidmans in the safety of our own rooms but clam up completely when faced with an audience? Part of the art of being an actor is to lose 'oneself' and become your character while totally forgetting there is an audience out there. If you are terribly self-conscious you may find this impossible to do. You may have a profound love for drama but a job in the profession that does not entail actually performing may be more suitable.

INABILITY TO COPE WITH PERFORMANCE PRESSURE

Most of the actors interviewed for this book admitted to getting first-night nerves at some point in their careers. In fact, some actors get nerves every night, ranging from a tightness in the chest and butterflies in the tummy to full-on nausea. Performance pressure can come on at any time during the run of a show. Daniel Day-Lewis walked out halfway through a performance of *Hamlet* at the National Theatre when the pressure got too much for him. Different people learn to cope in their own ways but if you think this could seriously affect your physical health and your emotional well-being, you might like to consider a role out of the limelight.

LACK OF PATIENCE

If only 25 per cent of actors are working at any one time, that means 75 per cent of them are sitting at home twiddling their thumbs. Actually, they are not, they are busy earning their living by doing other things and know that they have to keep plugging away in the industry to get results. Their mantra becomes 'be patient'. If you can't bear the thought of 'resting' for the majority of the time you may find the frustration is just too much and you'd be better off getting out of acting altogether and pursuing a different career.

SUSCEPTIBILITY TO DEPRESSION

It is tough when you keep getting rejected, when that role you *know* you are more than capable of filling goes to someone else. When the phone doesn't ring and you don't get called for audition it can hurt like crazy. But actors have to have the ability to bounce right back and try again, and again. If you find yourself giving way to depression and despair you will not be able to sustain yourself through long periods of 'resting' and the renewed chance of getting rejected again when you do go for audition. Your mental well-being is more important than any part, however big and if you know you have a tendency to become down-hearted and depressed you are going to have to seriously consider whether acting is for you.

'The best piece of advice I can give is to be true to yourself, and to know who you are. It is a very tough and competitive industry, and if you are armed with those two things, then you will be able to survive a lot longer than most.'

Jonathan Goodwin, professional magician, five TV's *Monkey Magic*

FASCINATING FACT

The market for London theatre audiences is estimated at £287 million. The West End contributes at least £220 million in sales, and theatres outside the West End are worth over £60 million. Overseas visitors buy around 30% of all theatre tickets.

Source: VisitBritain Survey of Visits to Visitor Attractions 2002

TANJA MCGHIE, 24, ACTRESS

'I'd wanted to go to drama school since I was about ten years old but when I sat down and worked out how much they cost I realised I didn't have enough money to go to the likes of Central. I contemplated doing a degree at university but in the end I plumped for the Academy Drama School because it was geared up to let you work and earn as you learned. The course is called the full-time Acting Evening Course and you work during the day and then the minimum amount of hours of study you have to do is between 6.30pm and 10.30pm every day, Monday to Friday, and then all day on Saturday. I trained for two years and there were two showcases at the end of the course and about 20 agents came to each showcase.

'I didn't get an agent out of that but I did eventually get work doing children's theatre and a lot of pantomime – which was good as it pays quite well. Not having an agent is hard though, you have to be so motivated to actively go and look for work you really have to rely on yourself. A lot of actors will tell you it is auditions that put them off, but for me the worst part is having to stay motivated all the time. Another hard thing is that the pay is so bad you really do have to do other work as well and it is hard to get back from a day's work and then sit at your computer writing off for acting jobs.

'I was only 19 when I started at drama school so I did bar work and I also worked as a tour guide which was great for my voice and self-confidence, but mostly I have done office work. It is still relatively easy to get general office work through temp agencies. The work may be dull but the pay is ok – you can get nine pounds an hour even if you don't have computer skills.

'Nothing I have ever done as a temp has ever made me as happy as when I am acting. I love the rehearsal period because the beginning of a run is always exciting. I'm quite proud to be in this profession so it always makes me feel happy and contented when I am in a production, no matter what it is. I'm just glad to be doing it. The problem is when you have to take really crappy day jobs because that can really make you despondent. But I certainly wouldn't consider giving up the acting. When you hit really low points you just have to remember how much effort you have put into it and try and remain positive. I just remember how great acting is when I'm actually doing it and I find that pulls me through.

'Apart from the lack of money or job security the thing I hate the most is the schmoozing you have to do to get jobs. It's not pleasant but in this business it really is a lot to do with whom you know. Another thing is, I still get terrible nerves, it's bizarre but they seem to get worse the longer the run goes on. Stage fright is one of the worst downsides to the business because you would rather be doing anything, even queuing at Tesco, than to be up there on that stage.

'Realistically, in five years' time I would like to have found an enjoyable day job that makes me feel good about myself and still be doing three or four shows a year that pay at least Equity minimum. I don't think I'll ever be constantly employed as an actress but three or four shows a year would be fine.'

FASCINATING FACT

The UK's largest ever independently financed film, *The Phantom Of The Opera*, was completed at Pinewood Studios in 2004. The film has a budget of over $80 million and is set to open in the US and UK in December 2004.
Source: *Screen International* magazine

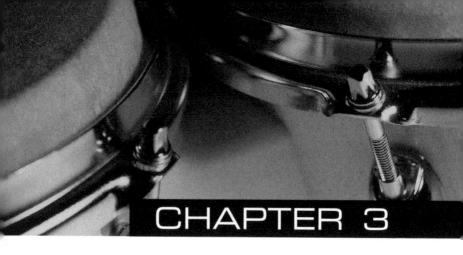

CHAPTER 3

Drama Queens (and Kings)

WHAT ARE THE JOBS?

So now you know a bit more about what skills you need to bring to the profession, but what could you actually do in the business? By now you may well have a very good idea about what an actor's job remit is, but the Jobs in Drama chart shown on page 11 may contain a few job titles you are unfamiliar with. Here's the low-down on the jobs in the profession.

PERFORMING

This is it; this is what most people who enter the performing arts strive to be – the performer, the person who takes on the role written down for them on the page. Actors and actresses appear in plays on stage, TV, radio and film. One day they could be reciting Shakespeare or Brecht, the next appearing in a soap such as *EastEnders* or *Hollyoaks*. They could be utilising other skills such as their singing and dancing in a West End musical such as *We Will Rock You*, or they could be doing something else entirely, perhaps a voice-over for a car advertisement, or a roleplay (they pretend to be a patient or a customer while a doctor or trainee learns how to deal with them). There are other types of performers in the profession as well, such as mime artists, magicians, stunt men, and presenters.

ADMINISTRATION/PRODUCTION

WRITING
Quite high up the 'food chain' in the world of drama is the playwright or scriptwriter (although many whinge that their contribution to the whole process is not appreciated enough). Without those words on the page the actors have nothing to work with – a bit like a potter with no clay. Some actors combine their performing role with that of the writer (Emma Thompson starred in *Sense and Sensibility* and also wrote the screen adaptation, while Richard O'Brien not only wrote *The Rocky Horror Show* but also starred in the stage and film versions). Many playwrights become household names, like Alan Bennett and David Hare and many also fill the dual roles of writer/director.

DIRECTING
It is the director's job to have an overall vision of what each theatrical piece will look and sound like when it is finally up there on the stage or screen. He or she will work closely with the actors to interpret the script to bring out its true meaning. A good director liaises with the set designer and lighting and sound crews so the production looks and sounds as they want it to. Some actors become directors (Clint Eastwood, Kenneth Branagh) and many people now study specifically to be directors at university and drama school. The director often works with an assistant director.

PRODUCTION
The role of producer or production manager may not sound very creative, but believe me, this is a job where you always have to flex those creative muscles! This is because producers are the money men and women: they have to work out just what everything is going to cost, make sure they have the finances in place to cover it and then bust a gut not to go over budget. This means they are coordinating all the different departments, making sure their work is finished on time so as not to accrue overtime bills. Some production managers work in-house, i.e. they are

employed by a particular theatre or theatre group, but most work freelance, especially in the film world where the producer's name is often as important as the director's (producer Jerry Bruckheimer's name can be seen on many big action movies such as *Bad Boys* and *Top Gun*). Also attached to the production office are the administrators, accountants and secretarial staff, and usually on the team somewhere will be a lawyer, sorting out contractual problems, royalties and rights.

BACKSTAGE/TECHNICIANS

STAGE MANAGER

One of the most important people backstage is the stage manager who acts as a communicator between the actors, the technical staff and any support crew who may also be involved. He or she is responsible for making sure the actors, musicians and dancers turn up to rehearsals and performances on time and know what they are doing, and that the props department, costumes, hair and make-up are also in the right place at the right time. This can be a logistical nightmare so anyone contemplating this role has to be able to take responsibility. They must have a logical, common-sense approach and not get panicked easily. On large shows with big casts the stage manager may employ the aid of an assistant stage manager.

SETTING THE SCENE

The set designer and prop buyer are the people responsible for the sometimes magical look of stage productions and films. If the director says he wants the action to be set within Aladdin's cave, they have to make sure that is what the director gets. Often they will be working under restrictions that will test their creativity to the full: at small theatre companies the budget may only be modest, or the stage area so cramped the set design will have to be modified to accommodate the props and the cast. They must also take into account safety considerations: the one thing they don't want on opening night is for the cast to be falling over the scenery, but such glitches are normally smoothed out at technical rehearsals.

Also working on the visual aspects of a production, be it TV, film or theatre are the costume designer, wardrobe department and hair and make-up. While the wardrobe department is responsible for the actual production and upkeep of the costumes, the costume designer draws the initial designs, oversees them as they are being made and refines them during the dress rehearsal when any problems can be sorted out. Hair and make-up is also an integral part of a production's look – everything from afro wigs and hippy face paint (from the show *Hair!*) to animal whiskers and fur (*Cats*).

LIGHTING AND SOUND

The lighting technicians are also important to the look of a production. By choosing various colours, filters and different strengths of light they can alter the feel and mood of the stage considerably. A large show may have a lighting designer working with a team of electricians, and on a film or TV set there is usually a lighting cameraman and riggers to set the lights up, while in small theatre groups all the lighting may be the responsibility of just one person. They have to coordinate closely with the set designer and once again, health and safety are an important part of their job. New technology has greatly increased the scope of what lighting technicians can achieve, but it also means they must keep abreast of the latest developments, especially in the computer software available.

The same can be said of the sound technicians who do everything from making sure the cast's microphones are working properly, to adding on all those evocative noises (an owl hooting, waves crashing to ground in the background) that can add so much to the atmosphere of a production. Again, new technology means many sounds can now be produced via computers.

Other backstage or technical jobs include special effects, continuity (most often in films and TV) and editor (again, mainly in film or TV).

SUPPORT STAFF

THE AGENT

They say that behind every big star there stands a good agent. However, finding one is never easy. Many agents attend the special graduation productions put on by the main drama schools each year and if you are a very lucky graduate, you could get an agent there. Others find clients through recommendations. Most budding actors find they need a body of work behind them before they can get themselves an agent. So why get one at all? Because having the name of an agent on your CV will make you look professional and as if you are taking your career seriously.

An agent is there to push you in the direction of good jobs and to steer you clear of anything dodgy. An agent should act as a mentor to you, advising you on the auditions you should be going to and to whom you should be talking. Unfortunately, it doesn't always work that way and many actors discover they actually generate more work themselves than they ever get through an agent. Agents earn their money by taking a percentage of the fee for every job they secure for you. This is usually around the 15 per cent mark.

'Never, ever, pay an agent to take you onto their books.'

Kate Gielgud, actress/voice coach

THE CASTING DIRECTOR

An agent is a good person to know, but not half as good as a casting director. On large productions the casting director is responsible for finding exactly the right actors for each of the roles available. This can be incredibly important when they are casting the lead roles because if they don't get it right, everyone is going to notice. Getting to know casting directors from auditions and read-throughs is good because even if you don't get one job, you may well come to mind when they are casting for another production. In some cases, agents will do deals with casting directors. If the agent has a big name actor the casting director wants the agent may negotiate so other actors on their books are considered for smaller roles in order for the casting director to secure the services of the star. In smaller theatre companies the director takes on the responsibility for casting.

FRONT OF HOUSE ROLES

While all the people above are plying their trades behind the scenes, out in front of house the theatre manager is sorting out the box office staff, the ushers and the bar staff. Their contributions are all important because they come into direct contact with the public and if you want people to come back again and again you must ensure their evening out is a pleasant experience, with efficient, polite staff making sure everything goes smoothly.

RELATED ROLES

Other jobs you may not have thought of are drama teacher or drama coach or voice coach, doing the publicity for a show by working in the press office, or what about becoming a drama therapist or even a film or theatre critic?

FASCINATING FACT

Westminster Council has just approved plans for producer Cameron Mackintosh to build a new 500 seater auditorium at the Queen's Theatre, Shaftesbury Avenue. A new flexible theatre called the Sondheim will open giving the Queen's 10% more seating than the National Theatre on the South Bank.

Source: *West End Extra* newspaper

ANDY SPIEGEL, ACTOR/CASTING DIRECTOR

Andy did a Performing Arts degree at Middlesex University with drama as his major and music and dance as his minors. He has worked pretty consistently ever since. When resting he works as a temp in the accounts department of a literary agency.

'Although I worked straight after finishing my degree I didn't get to play an adult until I was 26. I'm quite small and they like small people for jobs on children's TV because you seem non-threatening. I did *Sooty* for ITV and that proved to be a great job because I got loads of repeat fees for it. I've also done quite a lot of live work at places like the Nuffield Theatre in Southampton and at BAC in London and I toured the whole of Europe in a production of *Hair!* But the business is constantly changing and one of the biggest changes recently has been the amount of corporate work that is coming through. In the last ten years, big companies have started using actors for their major events more and more. These gigs can be very lucrative. I've been lucky enough in the past to play football with David Beckham on a McDonald's corporate job and been paid for the privilege. I've got another one with Siemens coming up at the Carlton Studios in Nottingham where I have to play a gangster and "kidnap" the Managing Director. Adverts can also earn you a lot of money. I did one for a Dutch telephone company and was paid almost two thousand pounds for a day's work.

'Nowadays you don't absolutely need an Equity card to work because the union rules are much easier now, but I would still say to any budding actors get your Equity card because it makes you look so much more professional. The same is also true of agents. I personally do not believe you can survive without an agent. It is important to find an agent you really get on with – you wouldn't believe how many actors are scared of their agents! Spotlight offers brilliant advice into which agents to go with. Another thing you really have to do is get yourself into Spotlight – it is absolutely essential. You need to get good photos done for that, which can be expensive but they are what you are judged on so you won't get in the door without them. A showreel is also important but again, it can be very expensive but you have to speculate to accumulate in acting because you are your product and if you are marketed well then you are going to get more work.

'A lot about acting is pure blag; many actors say that they've got away with it for 20 years. You need to have a lot of self-confidence and you need to have a thick skin. Some of us are more pragmatic about it, because you can't let it get to you. Nowadays it is much more about what you look like than what you can do, which is a terrible indictment on the way the industry has gone, but it is the truth. To be successful in this business you have to want it more than anything else so go out there and hustle, network, write letters, keep your ear to the ground and find out who is doing which shows because people move about. Read *The Stage* and keep in contact with the actors and casting directors you work with because networking is so important.

'One of the biggest downsides to the business is being out of work. It's easy to be an actor when you are working but the true crux to being an actor is when you are resting. There's a lot of disrespect to actors, we are known as very fickle, flighty and shallow because people don't see the amount of work we have to put in just to get a job. My advice is keep your hand in by doing a course or a rehearsed reading and go and see lots of shows. You also have to have other strings to your bow. The actors I know who are the most depressed and the most unfulfilled are the ones who sit at home waiting for that call to come through. This is a difficult life and it can make you neurotic because you never know where the next pay cheque is coming from. This aspect of the life means some people run out of steam and drop out.

'It is really important to know what your strengths are. If you are good at accents and voices then radio may be a good place for you to work. If you look good, have professional management and are talented then you have the formula to succeed. I know I'm not going to get fabulously wealthy through this, recently I did panto and all the actors got paid just £300 a week, but I have had some fantastic times.'

FASCINATING FACT

The first British film to win the Oscar for Best Film was *Hamlet* way back in 1948. The great British actor Sir Laurence Olivier not only starred in the film, he also directed and produced it.
Source: *Oscar: A Pictorial History*,
published by Associated Press

SHOW ME THE MONEY

HOW MUCH WILL YOU EARN?
For every megastar actor out there like Tom Cruise earning millions of dollars per movie there are dozens of others scraping a living together. The one thing you don't come into the business

for is to get rich. The preceding case study shows even an actor of many years' experience can find himself doing panto for the princely sum of just £300 a week. Obviously, some jobs pay more than others and if you are doing an advertisement or TV show or series where you get repeat fees the money can really add up over time. By law, the minimum weekly wage for 22-year-olds and over is now £4.50 per hour (£3.80 for 18- to 21-year-olds), but Equity has set its own minimum wages for its members. Of these, the lowest are obviously for work with small theatre companies, while one of the highest is for working with the BBC. At present if you work as an actor in a West End theatre the Equity minimum is £446 a week and if you are working in a small-scale theatre the minimum is £302 per week. Stage managers in the West End should get £480, while in small-scale theatres the sum is £310. Directors get paid an upfront fee and then a weekly fee. In the West End the amounts are £2,339 upfront and then a weekly fee of £175.43. Remember, these are only minimum guidelines; if you are a named star, guaranteed to pull in the crowds, your agent or manager will be able to negotiate your fee. Yet even huge stars such as Nicole Kidman and Gwyneth Paltrow agreed to be paid the Equity norm when they both appeared on the West End stage.

Courses for Horses

Before you ever get to earn any money as an actor, first you've got to train to be one. As stated before, not every actor working in this country has been to drama school but the great majority have.

WHAT'S ON OFFER?

Metier, The Sector Training Organisation for the Arts and Entertainment Industries, and Skillset, the industry organisation for training in film, TV, video and radio (see Resources) both offer comprehensive information on the wide range of NVQs (National Vocational Qualifications or SVQs in Scotland) you can now take in all the performing arts (from actor, to singer, and right up to director). Edexcel approves a number of First, National, and Higher National Diplomas and Certificates (HND, HNC) in everything from acting to make-up. These qualifications are the first step preparing you for higher education.

You can also do degree courses in drama at universities and colleges, but many of these tend to concentrate on the academic side of the subject rather than training you in the practical aspects of stagecraft. If you graduate from one of these courses and really want to enter the profession you can do a postgraduate course at a drama school. But if you are certain you want to act or work backstage, then a vocational course specifically designed to train you as a performer or stage manager/technician is what you should be aiming for. On these you will spend many hours a day doing practical work under the supervision of experts. So the first thing you should think about when considering which college or university you wish to attend is, am I actually going to use my training to be a performer, or do I just want to study performing arts because I'm interested and will then use the skills I learn to do something else in the future?

Although you can enter training later in life (many drama schools will accept applications from people between 25 and 30 years old) by so doing you will immediately rule yourself out of some acting parts because by the time you complete your course you are going to be too old to play a person in their late teens or early twenties! You'll also be a newly qualified actor in competition with experienced actors who are the same age as you but who have already worked in the profession for years. At most drama schools the minimum age for entry to a three-year course is 18, while entry age for one- or two-year courses is a minimum of 21.

'I'd recommend anyone to take a year off before starting on an acting course, just to get some life experience because the competition, pressure and depth of work at drama school is such you need to be older to survive. I did a secretarial course before going to RADA and it has proved invaluable.'

Kate Gielgud, actress/voice coach

Although training at a drama school can be very expensive (in some cases over £7,000 a year. At the Royal Academy of Dramatic Art (RADA) the fees for the three-year BA Acting degree are currently £3,586 per term, or a whopping £10,760 per year), places on these courses are always oversubscribed.

'At some (drama schools) the ratio of applicants to places is 50 to one.'

Source: 'A Practical Guide To Vocational Training in Dance And Drama', published by the National Council for Drama Training (NCDT) and the Council for Dance Education And Training (CDET)

Although there are no formal entry requirements to many drama courses if you can show you have a keen interest in the performing arts it will do your cause no harm whatsoever. Some courses will require the equivalent of five GCSEs/S grades and a few require two A-levels/three Scottish Highers or the equivalent. Other good qualifications to have are a BTEC National Diploma in Performing Arts, a Vocational A-level in Performing Arts and Entertainment Industries, or an SQA National Certificate in Dramatic Arts or Theatre Arts. These are the requirements at Mountview Theatre Academy but it also welcomes applications from people without standard entry qualifications.

GIVING YOURSELF THE ADVANTAGE

There are already lots of things you can do while still at school to give yourself an advantage over other applicants to drama school.

- Act as much as possible. In your school play, in community theatre or youth groups, or with your local amateur dramatic society – no matter how small the part, all experience is good experience.

- Show just how interested and keen on drama you are by attending as many live performances as possible. Write your own notes on each show, paying particular attention to what you thought of the acting performances.

- Read plays, in fact, read a large variety of plays – everything from Shakespeare to Strindberg, Oscar Wilde to

Tom Stoppard. Learn certain speeches by heart and discover what you feel most comfortable with – serious drama, tragedy or light comedy.

- If it is part of your school's curriculum take a GCSE in Drama or in Expressive Arts, or if you live in Scotland take a Higher or Advanced Higher in Drama.

- Join an amateur dramatic society in your area or, if you can afford to, take private drama lessons. Many young people between the ages of 13 and 21 join the National Youth Theatre (NYT). It offers courses at 13 centres around the country in acting, costume making, lighting and sound, prop making, and stage management and gives its members a real taste of what it is like to work in theatre as well as teaching them practical skills. NYT has an audition hotline on 0845 903 9063 (for more information on NYT see Resources).

- For a list of other amateur drama clubs and regional youth theatres contact The National Association of Youth Theatres at naytuk@aol.com (for more information on NAYT see Resources). The National Council for Drama Training also has an information sheet on youth theatre (see Resources).

- Contact your local theatre and see if it is possible to do some work experience with them. Even acting as an usher will give you a feel of the theatre experience.

- Start reading the drama reviews in your local press as well as in national newspapers. Buy *The Stage* newspaper occasionally to get a feel for the profession (see Resources).

- If you are interested in the technical aspects of theatre then start designing and making your own models, props, costumes, masks, etc. to show you have ability as well as an interest.

Most drama schools are looking for raw talent and enthusiasm, so entry is usually via one or more auditions. Some schools ask for a monologue from a play by Shakespeare or another Jacobean playwright plus a piece in clear contrast to the first. Others will ask for an improvisation. There may well be an audition fee of £30. You will also need to go for interview so the more knowledgeable and enthusiastic about acting you are, the better.

ON COURSE
Typically, a three-year BA Acting or Performance course will cover the following areas:

Voice, movement, and physical skills
You will develop your range, projection, strength and flexibility. You may well study Alexander Technique and, if part of the course, study music theory and develop your singing and dancing.

Acting skills
You may learn Stanislavsky-based acting exercises, do improvisations and 'in-house' presentations including classical and modern texts. By year three you will appear in public productions with invited agents and casting directors in the audience.

Add-on skills
Add-ons such as **stage combat** (both armed and unarmed), and **tumbling** may be included in your course.

Technical skills
All acting and performance degree students will be introduced to **technical crafts** as well as **radio, microphone** and **television technique**. Some courses also provide **front of house** training.

Masterclass workshops
Throughout the course students will attend specialist workshops with professionals from the industry.

Audition technique
Finally, in order to get those all-important jobs, students will be trained to select suitable audition pieces and to present themselves appropriately to prospective employers.

Sources: Mountview Academy of Theatre Arts and RADA

ON COURSE
Typically, a two-year BA or Graduate Diploma in Theatre Technical Arts will include:

Stage management
This will involve elements of **score reading, text analysis, theatre history, production** and **company management**, as well as **first aid,** and **health and safety** at work.

Design skills
Areas covered include **set design, prop making, wardrobe, printing,** and **scenic painting**. The skills learned here will be as applicable to exhibitions, trade shows and conferences as to TV, video, film or live theatre.

Construction skills
Construction is becoming increasingly technical and so you must learn **computer aided design** alongside the more traditional skills of technical **drawing, metalwork** and **wood turning**.

Lighting and sound
You will learn basic **electrics** along with the more technical **board operation, lighting design** and **sound design**.

By year two you will be working full time on productions for presentation to the public.

Sources: Mountview Academy of Theatre Arts, and RADA

If you decide you would like a career teaching drama in the state system, you will first have to graduate and then take a course leading to a Postgraduate Certificate in Education (PGCE) in order to qualify as a teacher. You can get more information on becoming a drama teacher from the Society of Teachers of Speech and Drama (see Resources).

WHICH WAY NOW?
By now you should be clearer on what kind of course you want to apply for. If you do decide to go the vocational route, then the National Council for Drama Training (NCDT) accredits the following courses at 21 different colleges.

SCHOOL	COURSE/S	TYPE OF FUNDING
Academy of Live and Recorded Arts (ALRA)	1 Year Acting 3 Year Acting	DaDA* DaDA
Arts Educational (ArtsEd)	1 Year Acting 3 Year Acting	DaDA DaDA
Birmingham School of Speech and Drama	1 Year Acting 3 Year Acting	State Funded HE State Funded HE
Bristol Old Vic Theatre School	2/3 Year Acting 2/3 Year Stage Management	State Funded HE State Funded HE
Central School of Speech and Drama	3 Year Acting 3 Year Stage Management	State Funded HE State Funded HE
Drama Centre	3 Year Acting	State Funded HE
Drama Studio	1 Year Acting	Full Fees/Independent
East 15 Acting School	1 Year Acting 3 Year Acting	Full Fees/Independent State Funded HE

SCHOOL	COURSE/S	TYPE OF FUNDING
Guildford School of Acting (GSA)	1 Year Acting/Musical Theatre	DaDA
	1 Year Stage Management	DaDA
	2 Year Stage Management	DaDA
	3 Year Acting	DaDA
	3 Year Musical Theatre	DaDA
Guildhall School of Music and Drama	3 Year Acting	State Funded HE
	3 Year Stage Management	State Funded HE
Italia Conti Academy of Theatre Arts Ltd	3 Year Acting	—
London Academy of Music and Dramatic Art (LAMDA)	3 Year Acting	DaDA
	2 Year Stage Management	DaDA
Manchester Metropolitan University School of Theatre	3 Year Acting	State Funded HE
Mountview Academy of Dramatic Arts	1 Year Acting/Musical Theatre	DaDA
	2 Year Stage Management	DaDA
	3 Year Acting	DaDA
	3 Year Acting/Musical Theatre	DaDA
Oxford School of Drama	1 Year Acting	DaDA
	3 Year Acting	DaDA
Queen Margaret University College	3 Year Acting	State Funded HE
	3 Year Stage Management	State Funded HE
Rose Bruford College	3 Year Acting	State Funded HE
	3 Year Stage Management	State Funded HE
	3 Year Costume	State Funded HE
	3 Year Scenic Arts	State Funded HE
	3 Year Lighting	State Funded HE
Royal Academy of Dramatic Art (RADA)	3 Year Acting	State Funded HE
	2 Year Stage Management	State Funded HE

SCHOOL	COURSE/S	TYPE OF FUNDING
Royal Scottish Academy of Music and Drama (RSAMD)	3 Year Acting 3 Year Stage Management	State Funded HE State Funded HE
Royal Welsh College of Music and Drama	1 Year Acting 1 Year Stage Management 3 Year Acting 3 Year Stage Management	Full Fees/Independent Full Fees/Independent State Funded HE State Funded HE
Webber Douglas Academy of Dramatic Art	1 Year Acting 3 year Acting	DaDA State Funded HE

*DaDA stands for Dance and Drama Awards Scheme

Source: NCDT. For contact information on the above colleges you can contact NCDT direct or refer to *The Complete Guide To Performing Arts Courses 2005*, published by Trotman – see Resources

FUNDING YOUR STUDIES

You will already have read about how expensive drama school training can be. This is because the courses tend to be very intensive and require input from a large number of professional teachers covering the different disciplines. However, don't panic yet and think you won't be able to afford it. As you can see from the above chart, there are three main ways the courses can be funded.

STATE-FUNDED HE COURSES

At present, students entering higher education pay an upfront student fee contribution of £1,125 per year towards the cost of their course. Under proposed new government policy this is to rise to up to £3,000 per year in 2006 (to be paid on graduation). However, students from lower income backgrounds can apply for help with this fee and can also apply for student loans to cover living costs (at present the maximum loan is £4,000). For more information on Higher Education funding, the Department for Education and Skills (DfES) publishes a guide, *Financial Support*

For Higher Education Students, which is available from the DfES Information Line on 0800 731 9133. (For more information on DfES see Resources.)

DANCE AND DRAMA AWARDS (DaDA)

DaDAs were first introduced in 1999 and they help students wishing to take approved vocational courses at independent drama schools with their fees and maintenance. But you should be aware the awards only go to the most talented students and up to 40 per cent of students on these courses have to fund their own places. The DfES has a DaDA information booklet. Contact the DfES publication line on 0845 6022260 or at www.dfes.gov.uk/dancedrama.

Each drama school is itself responsible for allocating these awards. Your financial circumstances as well as your ability may be taken into consideration, but only as a secondary factor. DaDA students may apply for help with their student fee contribution, but they cannot apply for student loans. However, they can apply for hardship grants to help with their maintenance costs.

In England, Scotland and Wales, Manchester Education Authority processes applications for DaDA fees and maintenance. Contact the telephone enquiry service on 0161 234 7021 or write to:
The Chief Education Officer,
Student Support Section,
PO Box 191
Manchester M3 3ST
Email: Fund4study@notes.manchester.gov.uk

If you live in Northern Ireland you should contact:
The Department for Higher and Further Education Training and Employment,
39–49 Adelaide House,
Adelaide Street,
Belfast
BT2 8FD
Tel: 02890 257 735

Some courses do not attract state sector funding and for these you will be responsible for the full cost of the fees plus your own maintenance costs as you are not eligible for a loan or a grant.

FULL COST OR INDEPENDENT COURSES

Most of the courses where you will have to find the full fees yourself are postgraduate courses or those aimed at mature students. If you are on a DaDA-funded course but fail to win a DaDA you will also have to fund the course yourself and pay your maintenance costs. Over a three-year course this can add up to as much as £50,000, but do not despair, there are still alternative forms of funding out there.

Some students may be able to get a Career Development Loan (CDL) from a high street bank, where the DfES pays the interest on the loan for the length of your course. You then start paying the repayment instalments up to five months after graduation. You can get a CDL pack by contacting the DfES on 0800 585 505 or from www.lifelonglearning.co.uk.

SCHOLARSHIPS AND BURSARIES

Every student wanting to study the performing arts at a drama, music or dance school should contact their preferred schools *as early as possible*. That's because many of them have specially endowed awards schemes such as scholarships and bursaries to help students with their course fees, but you have to hurry because they are over-subscribed and only the most talented students get them. For example, RADA offers both scholarships and bursaries (acting course only) to support students in genuine financial need. At Mountview they have a number of different scholarships including the Dame Judi Dench Scholarship, the Sir John Mills Scholarship, and the Somerset Scholarship. In order to find out more about what scholarships are available you should contact drama colleges direct.

If all else fails and you are still short of funding you can apply to charitable trusts and foundations for help. This can be a long and time-consuming exercise but if you want it enough it can be found. Check your local reference library for a copy of the *Directory of Grant-Making Trusts*, published by Charities Aid Foundation. You should also look out for *University Scholarships and Awards* by Brian Heap, published by Trotman. Alternatively, check out www.fundfinder.org.uk/index.php or www.scholarship-search.org.uk.

AMBER EDLIN, 30, DANCER-TURNED-ACTRESS
Amber started dance classes at the age of four at the Hillingdon Theatre Dance School and reached a high level of proficiency. She also joined a youth drama group at The Beck Theatre in Hayes and although she loved dancing she found acting more enjoyable because it combined studying text and performing. When she realised that she did not have the physicality to be a ballerina she applied to attend Guildford School of Acting on their three-year acting course. Since graduating she has toured in *The Misanthrope*, appeared on the West End stage and on TV in such series as *London's Burning* and *EastEnders*.

'I didn't get a good agent immediately after I graduated and so I spent a lot of time doing fringe performances and writing off for lots of jobs. During this time I learned which venues agents will go to and which they won't to spot new talent. Getting a good agent in this business is very difficult unless you have some sort of personal contact who will recommend you. Once I got a good agent I felt things start to shift and went to castings more frequently.

'What I love most about acting is I am doing something I love and getting paid for it. Some days I come out of castings, especially those for commercials, and think "hang on a minute, most people are typing or serving customers and I have just been pretending to see thousands of zombies, or eat a bowl of pasta, or react to an imaginary dog". It's madness! The worst thing is the "resting" aspect, which can be soul destroying. In between gigs you have to get another job and I have done everything from waitressing, to teaching dance and working as a temp. It can get very frustrating because it is not what you want to do and more often than not it is not very stimulating.

'Professionally, I wish producers were a bit bolder with new names. You see the same people on TV all the time and I wish they would take more chances. I do understand that names draw audiences but come on, take a risk! In my ideal world I would play a regular character in a fantastically written sitcom or drama series (that would be lovely for the security). However, in reality, I may have to take matters into my own hands and start writing my own scripts.

'I would encourage young people to learn the skills if they really enjoy acting but they need to go into it with their eyes open to the difficulties because there seem to be more and more of us and less and less work! However, if they really have set their heart on it I would say "be confident, and GO FOR IT!"'

Finally, in this section on drama, just to prove not every dramatic person is necessarily an actor, here's someone making a living in performing arts but doing something very different indeed.

STUART SCOTT, 27, PART-TIME PROFESSIONAL MAGICIAN
After graduating from university Stuart decided not to follow the conventional graduate route. As he had always been interested in magic and magic tricks, he went to work with a German youth circus, after which he performed in two stores in London before working in Africa. Stuart still performs magic to earn extra money but on an informal basis.

'Being a professional magician was never something I wanted to do as a career but I had always been interested in magic, both as a performance art and as a mental discipline (inventing illusions involves great skill in lateral thinking). While I was at school I joined a circus club and learned a variety of related performance skills including juggling, unicycling, and stilt walking. I learned magic tricks from books and through lots of practice. I also invented effects that I then performed and really the best learning came from the performing. My training was informal and a lot of fun, but training is no substitute to actually performing and learning from experience.

'Getting gigs as a magician can be difficult, especially in off-seasons. Also, getting to a good standard can take a long time and requires dedication and a lot of patience. I'd say to anyone who is seriously considering it as a career perform as often as you can to as many different types of audience as you can. Develop your skills rather than rely on props and don't try to copy other people, develop your own style. In fact, I'd say rather than buy props buy books on magic and devise at least one unique act and then practise it until you can do it perfectly. I'd also urge them to join a magic club to meet other magicians – you should ask their advice, but not always take it! It's also good to broaden your horizons in the performing arts. I have written, produced, acted, directed and been a theatre manager.

'Magic has gone through major changes in the UK in the last five years. In the nineties there was next to no magic on TV in the UK other than Paul Daniels. Now there has been a revival in magic brought about in part by David Blaine's first TV special and also by renewed interest in magic itself through the *Harry Potter* books and films. TV raises audiences' expectations of the performer and magicians are going to have to rise to that. There's a lot of imitation but that's because of a lack of imagination on the part of some performers. It is hard to keep up with the best magicians shown on TV but magic has the advantage of being even more impressive performed live!

'One of the best things about doing what I do is meeting people and giving them an experience they may remember for the rest of their lives. Magic is a very powerful art. A trick you've performed a thousand times in the past may be commonplace to you, but it may have a profound effect on your audience. I will always be a magician. It's more a way of seeing the world than just something you do.'

CHAPTER 5

Let's Face the Music

MUSIC UNCOVERED

It's a harmless daydream many of us indulge in from time to time: winning a TV reality show such as *Pop Idol* or *Fame Academy* and going on to have an enormously successful (and highly lucrative) career in the music business. Unfortunately, for the vast majority of us it will always remain a dream, but if your interest in music goes beyond that of just being a fan there are plenty of jobs you can do within this sphere that may not make you rich and famous, but will definitely give you a fulfilling and rewarding career.

> **FASCINATING FACT**
>
> The resurgence of guitar-led bands such as The Strokes and The Darkness has led to an increase in guitar sales. UK electric guitar sales rose by nearly 25% in 2002.

WHAT ARE THE JOBS?

Obviously, the people who are most visible in the music industry are the performers we see on our TV screens, in videos and at concerts. They are opera singers like Pavarotti, rock bands such as

The Darkness, easy-listening artists such as Nora Jones, or they play in orchestras such as the London Symphony Orchestra. Less visible performers include the session musicians who play the music on ads and jingles, band members in musical theatre shows such as *We Will Rock You* or *Mamma Mia!* and even high-profile DJs such as Moby or Fat Boy Slim. Only people with great talent and skill can make it as professional performers, be it as pianists, violinists or singers. If you have made up your mind to be a performer you should already be playing an instrument or having singing lessons and taking graded examinations. In fact, in order to train as a classical musician you will need Grade 8 on your main instrument and Grade 6 on a second instrument. In the world of popular music no such criteria exist and some people do make it without formal training, but these are the exception rather than the rule.

If you don't have the talent or inclination to be a performer there are still many things you can do in the music world. The music business is huge in terms of both scale and monetary value – in fact, the annual figures from the British Phonographic Industry (BPI) show that in 2002 sales of DVDs, CDs and cassettes had a total market value of £1.18 billion, and that's before taking into account the ticket sales for live concerts, or revenues from the sale of sheet music or instruments, and from merchandise such as T-shirts. So, you could work in a music shop selling guitars, or you could even make guitars. You could write songs or be a music journalist, work for a music publisher's office or even become a manager like Simon Cowell with your own roster of artists. Listed in the chart below are just some of the many jobs in the music industry that you can train to do.

SPOTLIGHT ON LORD ANDREW LLOYD WEBBER

For over 30 years Andrew Lloyd Webber's musical theatre shows have been wowing audiences all over the world and he is one of our most successful and well-known composers.

- His *Phantom of the Opera* is the largest grossing piece of musical theatre in the world. It has a worldwide box office of more than £3 billion.

JOBS IN THE MUSIC INDUSTRY

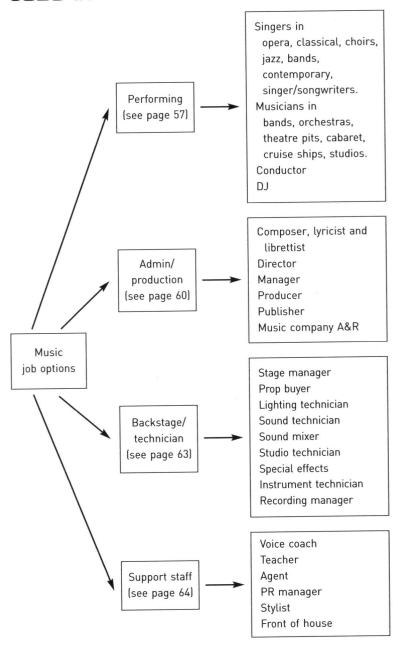

Music job options

Performing (see page 57)

Singers in
   opera, classical, choirs,
   jazz, bands,
   contemporary,
   singer/songwriters.
Musicians in
   bands, orchestras,
   theatre pits, cabaret,
   cruise ships, studios.
Conductor
DJ

Admin/ production (see page 60)

Composer, lyricist and
   librettist
Director
Manager
Producer
Publisher
Music company A&R

Backstage/ technician (see page 63)

Stage manager
Prop buyer
Lighting technician
Sound technician
Sound mixer
Studio technician
Special effects
Instrument technician
Recording manager

Support staff (see page 64)

Voice coach
Teacher
Agent
PR manager
Stylist
Front of house

- More than 125 million copies of albums composed and/or produced by Lloyd Webber have been sold worldwide.

- He has won an Oscar, a Golden Globe, 7 Tony Awards, 5 Laurence Olivier Awards, 3 Grammys, 14 Ivor Novellos, and numerous other awards.

- In 1991 he was the first and only composer to have six productions running at one time in the West End.

- In 2004, after an absence of 18 years, Michael Crawford is to return to the West End stage to star in Lloyd Webber's newest show, a musical version of the famous Wilkie Collins novel, *The Woman In White*.

Source: The Really Useful Group

WHEN YOU KNOW THE NOTES TO SING

IS THE MUSIC INDUSTRY FOR YOU?

Music is everywhere these days – if it's not pouring out of your CD player, radio or TV set, then it's being piped through shopping malls and lifts, or you are downloading it onto your computer or mobile telephone. Someone, somewhere, has to compose that music, play it and record it. The public usually only sees the glamorous face of the music business in the form of the performers up there on stage, be they playing a violin concerto or a piece of rock music, but many of the jobs within the industry are unglamorous and extremely hard work. As in the acting world there are some aspects of the music industry you need to have a long think about before deciding this is the world for you.

INSECURITY

Of the approximately 2,150 people who graduated from music studies in 2002, only 54 per cent went straight into employment, and of these only 34 per cent went into full-time paid work in the UK (data supplied by the Higher Education Statistics Agency (HESA)). This means there are a lot of music graduates out there who did not find work. The music world is notoriously fluid and fickle, so a particular job in music will not necessarily be 'for life'. You must be prepared to move around from job to job and to sustain periods of unemployment. If you are a performer you may have to teach or do session work in order to supplement your earnings. If you work in other areas of the industry, such as a record company, you may well find yourself frequently moving around departments and from concentrating on one artist to another. This certainly makes life challenging, but not everybody enjoys such insecurity and instability in their working lives. If you would like a more structured career you should seriously think about jobs that may be connected to the industry but are less closely linked to the performing side.

LOW INCOME
We will explore the money you can make in music in more detail in Chapter 6, where you will find a box listing some of the huge sums of money musicians can earn, but you should be aware that these are the people at the top of their profession. For every Yehudi Menuhin, Charlotte Church or Darkness there are countless struggling violinists, opera singers or rock groups earning fairly low wages. For instance, if you are a musician in an orchestra, the annual rate of pay starts at around £13,500. If you work as a freelancer you may be contracted to do a very lucrative tour for six months of the year and then not work again for a further three months. Although the potential for earning a good wage should be important to you, the primary reason you should be in this business is because you love it. There is too much competition for jobs in this industry for you to make a success of it if you don't feel passionately about what you do.

BOREDOM
You may think boredom is a strange thing to bring up when discussing the exciting world of music, but jobbing musicians will tell you boredom can seriously affect the enjoyment they get from what they do. For example, say you are employed playing guitar in a band that is hired out for parties, weddings, bar mitzvahs and corporate dos. You will have a repertoire of songs you perform and not only will you rehearse these songs intensely but also you will end up playing the same songs night after night. There are only so many times you can play 'Lady In

Red' before it ceases to thrill you. This is particularly true when the music you are playing is not to your own personal taste. Playing the same pieces many times over can sap your enthusiasm and so you really have to be dedicated for it not to affect your performances adversely.

'If you have a family and a pension and a mortgage then the boredom of playing the same thing week in, week out on a long-running show in the West End is only offset by the knowledge you are financially secure.'

Carlton Edwards, Musical Director

ANTISOCIAL HOURS

No one working in the performing arts area can expect to work a standard 9 to 5, it just isn't like that. Performers tend to work while the public enjoys its leisure hours, this means in the evenings and at weekends. Even if you are a session musician working in a studio, you will often carry on playing until you get it right, which could be well into the night, and the same goes for bands recording their albums. You could be on tour so, on top of the hours you put in performing, you will also have to take into account the hours spent on the road getting from venue to venue. Non-performers such as A&R (Artist and Repertoire) scouts, roadies, tour managers, and press officers have to work around the performers so they too will be putting in long and often anti-social hours. If you want to be at home in time to put your feet up and watch your favourite TV soap each night, then this is definitely the wrong industry for you.

FASCINATING FACT

More than 150,000 legal downloads were sold in January 2003, outstripping vinyl, cassettes and DVD singles for the first time.

Source: Official UK Charts Company

MAKING MUSIC

If none of the above puts you off making a career for yourself in the music business, then you already have one of the personal attributes that will help you be a success – determination – and there are other strengths, both personal and physical, that will help you get on. It goes without saying that natural ability and talent are two key attributes for musical performers. Others include:

SOCIABILITY

Even if you are a solo artist, such as a singer/songwriter, you are going to need other people around you to help you make the music you want to. This is especially true if you are in an orchestra, a jazz band, a choir or any other form of group. You need to have good people skills, be able to interact and get on easily with other people. Life on the road, when you are touring, can get really intense so if you can keep a smile on your face and not fall out with people you will be an asset rather than a pain.

'Because it is a small, close world in the musical theatre end of the business, musicians, singers, dancers, choreographers and directors tend to go from show to show so you can't afford to make enemies. Because I'm personable, can get on with people and am well liked people want to keep on hiring me.'

Carlton Edwards, Musical Director

CREATIVITY

In the music world you really do have to 'think outside of the box'. If you are a songwriter or composer you will be using your creativity each and every day. A music manager will have to spot trends and think of imaginative ways to market his or her acts, and music teachers must come up with novel methods to keep their pupils interested and motivated.

STAMINA

Don't be fooled into thinking the music industry is all about having a lark, this is a serious business and in order to make it you are going to have to work long and hard. You have to put in the hours of practice, you may have to play every night, and the work is often exhausting (just imagine the concentration needed to play live Philip Glass's opera piece 'Einstein On The Beach', which lasts 5 hours). You need to be physically fit and mentally alert so you are going to have to look after yourself.

COMPUTER SKILLS

Many musicians now write and record music using software packages such as CUBASE so you need to be computer literate. This is especially true if you want to be a keyboard player, a sequencer, remixer or DJ where you will be sampling sounds electronically. Record companies have websites for their artists and for such things as back catalogue, while many ticket agencies such as Ticketmaster now accept bookings for concerts via the Internet, so make sure your computer skills are up to scratch.

ORGANISATIONAL SKILLS

Putting on any kind of musical performance can be a logistical nightmare, so the last thing anyone needs is for you to be disorganised. You need to be in certain places at certain times, you need to have practised until you are perfect, and you need to know what the people around you are also doing, so get yourself sorted! There is too much money involved in the business for things to go wrong; if you can help things run smoothly by having good organisational skills then people will be more inclined to employ you time and time again.

COMMON SENSE

Being level headed and having your feet placed firmly on the ground are great strengths to possess whatever career in music you plan to have. This is a fast-moving, often stressful world where people work under pressure. If you can keep your wits about you, stay calm and think things through logically, then people will know they can rely on you in a crisis. Creative people sometimes have a reputation for flakiness; make sure you have a reputation for using your common sense and you'll go far.

TEAM WORK

You really have to be a team player to get ahead in music. Basically, this is because so many roles within the music industry depend on working with other people. Music groups work as a team, roadies work as a team, and your management group *is* your team. You will need good communication skills and the ability to take orders as well as give them. The higher up the ladder of responsibility you get the more you have to learn to delegate and if you have a good working relationship with those around you they will be more inclined to share the burden of responsibility with you.

FASCINATING FACT

English National Opera (ENO) specialises in popular opera in the English language and has just had a £41 million facelift of its Coliseum theatre in London. The auditorium now holds 2,400 seats with perfect sightlines.

WILL YOU MAKE THE GRADE?

Just as there are strengths that will help you achieve your ambitions in music, so too are there weaknesses that could hold you back. Once again, this section is primarily aimed at performers and those in the positions closest to them. As you move away from this core group, these weaknesses become less relevant so if you do suffer from any of the following, you could still work in the music industry but in non-performance-related roles.

TONE DEAFNESS

We would all like to believe we have perfect pitch but the unfortunate fact is the majority of us don't. If you can't hold a tune to save your life, let alone find middle C, you probably already know making music is not for you. This is as true for people who play musical instruments as it is for singers because they very often 'play by ear' rather than read music. Although there is, apparently, a current trend for R&B and hip hop acts to be out of tune (e.g. Lumidee and Outkast's Andre 3000) there is no guarantee this fad will last any longer than other musical fads.

PERFORMANCE STRESS

If the thought of going out on stage and performing in front of thousands of people brings you out in a cold sweat there's little chance of you ever appearing at the Glastonbury Festival or the Brit Awards. Panic attacks and nerves will seriously affect your ability to perform – the vocal chords become constricted and you'll suddenly find you are playing with two left hands. Some people find that although they simply can't perform in front of a live audience, they are fine in a recording studio or orchestra pit where the audience can't see them. Others find performance stress becomes less of a problem or disappears completely the more they perform live. If you are in a school band take the opportunity to appear in as many shows or competitions as possible; this will give you an indication of whether nerves are going to get the better of you or not.

PRONENESS TO INJURY

Musicians really need to look after themselves. The human voice must be nurtured and nursed as serious throat infections or conditions such as nodules on the vocal chords can ruin promising singing careers (Julie Andrews of *Mary Poppins* and *The Sound of Music* has been told she must never sing again because of nodules). Most musicians play their instruments with their hands so they have to be careful to watch out for such conditions as RSI (repetitive strain injury) and arthritis and try their hardest not to damage them. Carlton Edwards had to give up the idea of becoming a concert pianist after two injuries to his hands (falling through a cold frame and a plate glass window), although he still works in the industry (see case study below).

LACK OF SELF-ESTEEM

This is an industry that can really knock your self-confidence for six. What if nobody likes the songs you sing or the music you make? If you go up to audition for a part in the latest musical in the West End with ten other performers and don't even get into the chorus line you can start to doubt your own ability. DON'T! Once you start to doubt yourself you won't have the confidence to convince others of your talents and skills. Self-belief is all in this game: remember, the product you are marketing is you, so go out there with the hard sell.

FASCINATING FACT

In the year 2000, 17,800 non-classical concerts were held at venues with a capacity of less than 5,000; 620 concerts were held at venues with a capacity of more than 5,000 and 229 outdoor shows were held.

Source: 'Counting The Notes'
The 2002 National Music Council (NMC) report

CARLTON EDWARDS,
MUSICAL DIRECTOR/COMPOSER

Carlton started playing the piano at the age of four. He was set to do a Music and Drama degree at Hull University and took a year out to work in London before starting the course. Here he found employment playing the piano in hotel foyers and also in private clubs and so he never took up his university place. Since then he has worked in the music industry constantly, first writing for a jingle company, performing his own songs, playing piano for rehearsals and more recently as Assistant Musical Director on West End shows such as *Oliver!*, *Mamma Mia!*, *Chitty Chitty Bang Bang* and *The Full Monty*.

'Writing for the jingle company was brilliant because it gave me both studio and engineering experience with sequencers and drum machines. I think everyone in the business should be learning new crafts within their sphere – there is always something new you can learn. That experience taught me my backstage skills are far better than my performing on stage skills and so I went on a tour of Canada with a group of students from a theatre school where I acted as musical director (MD), playing piano and making sure the cast were all singing in tune and looking after themselves. After that, a friend who was the MD on *Oliver!* rang to ask me to play the piano in the rehearsals when they had a cast change and the new cast members had to learn all their song parts and dance steps. From there I went on a tour of Canada with *Oliver!* and that is where I started to conduct the show and when I got back to England I went on to become assistant MD on *Mamma Mia!*

'The assistant MD usually plays the piano in the band in the pit and will normally play for six of the eight shows a week and then conduct the other two shows a week. He or she also has responsibility for rehearsals so you are always in the building and always busy. It can be enjoyable but it is pretty full on because you tend to have to pick up the pieces other people don't want to do. I like MDing – I like actors, I like people and I like working with music. For most of us who work in the West End, our days are free and once the show is up and running and you are comfortable with the performance side then you do have time for other things but one of the downsides of the job is that the hours are all round the wrong way. Some people take to working in the evenings but some do not. You have to be a nocturnal person. There is also performance pressure, and fear of failure because if you are MDing a show for people's entertainment then you want to make it as good as possible and that is stressful. It can be terrifying doing a show in a 2,000-seat theatre but you have to get over your fear otherwise it just becomes a nightmare in your head. What you have to say to yourself is this is just a theatre and it's just a band and everyone is helping each other. The worst that could happen is that the show stops – you're not packing parachutes.

'For this job you absolutely have to have people-management skills. It's all about social skills and pastoral care because to make the show successful you have to make sure your band is happy and your cast stays healthy. That's why a good MD always puts themselves last in the equation because if you are good at your job then you are strong enough and emotionally sorted enough to take on board the things that go wrong. Being a good musician is not enough, you have to be a psychiatrist, nursemaid and all round people person as well.

'Obviously, MDing is a full-time job, but you often find musicians have other outlets for their talents. I do a lot of youth work during the days and other people I know do gigs or concerts and they teach as well. It's really good for young people to have musicians who are actually working in the business teaching them because you know what is going on.

'Whatever you end up doing, you have to take it seriously, have fun but work hard and above all, practise! This career really is a vocation because it is so linked in with your hobby and pastimes and interests. If you are a good musician working in the industry you really will have to love what you do which means choosing your jobs carefully. Getting a job on a show with a long run may be financially secure but it can become boring playing the same thing week in and week out. I've seen some very good players lose their self-esteem because they hate the music they are playing every night. However, if you are adaptable, have ability and are realistic it really can be a financially and personally rewarding job.'

JOBS IN THE MUSIC INDUSTRY

You should have a good idea by now of what it takes to be a success in the music industry and you may know exactly which job within the industry you want. If you haven't started playing an instrument already or taking singing lessons, then becoming a performer may be extremely difficult, especially in classical music. However, this industry is huge and there are plenty of other careers you can pursue in music. The chart on page 47 listed a few of the job options available, and here we look at some of them in more detail.

PERFORMING

You can basically break down musical performers into two groups: **MUSICIANS** and **SINGERS**.

MUSICIANS

Musicians need to be extremely competent players. There are five main categories of instruments: brass, keyboard, percussion, strings, and wind, and some musicians play more than one instrument and also sing (Sting can play guitar and double bass). Most professional musicians need to be able to sight-read music, especially those working in orchestras. You could be a pianist, a drummer, or a violin player and the range of groups, bands and orchestras you can play in is astonishing. On the classical side there are extremely large symphony orchestras, or the orchestras attached to opera or ballet companies, string quartets, chamber groups and ensembles. Only very exceptional players have the talent and the emotional strength to become soloists. Many musicians working in classical music are employed on a freelance or contract basis where the contracts can run for one tour or a number of years.

On the popular music side the range is even greater, because 'popular' covers everything from jazz, folk and country to rap, soul and pop. You can play in large swing bands, rock groups and jazz quartets. You can also play in a military band or in the pit for musical theatre. You could be a session musician who spends the whole time working in a recording studio doing everything from jingles to guest appearing on someone else's album. Again, many are freelance. In the 2002 Census, 29,378 people stated they were working as musicians who were employees, while 24,967 stated they were self-employed musicians (these figures also include singers). As a musician you can expect to work in a variety of different locations including practice rooms, studios, jazz clubs, music halls and auditoriums, and if you are part of a show band you may well perform in marquees at weddings, parties and big events.

SINGERS

Singers also have a lot of job opportunities open to them. On the classical side there are choirs, and opera and operetta companies. You can be part of the chorus (the main body of singers), or you can be a soloist. Once again, soloists must have exceptional talent and will spend years training their voice. Popular music vocalists may or may not have had traditional vocal training and either sing as part of a band, as backing singers, or as soloists. Many singers are also musicians such as Chris Martin (Coldplay), Tori Amos and Jamie Cullum who all sing and play piano. Some specialise in session work in studios, while most will mix live work at concerts with a recording career.

Other performers include DJs, who remix records by other people at live events and in clubs. Many have no traditional musical training at all, but they need to have expert computer skills and be up to date with technology that is changing rapidly. For instance, most DJs used to use vinyl records to do their mixes, but new CD mixers are now taking over. Fat Boy Slim, Moby and Judge Jules are just some of the DJs earning very large sums for their services. You might not think of a conductor as being a performer but there he or she is, up on stage waving the baton. Many conductors are actually musicians with many years' experience. They will choose the pieces an orchestra plays and are there to rehearse the orchestra and on performance nights, to ensure the orchestra is in time, on the beat and is conveying the right emotions through the music. They have to be able to sight read and have a deep understanding of music theory.

Tastes in popular music are said to have a seven-year cycle. Three of the biggest trends in the last few years have been: the renaissance of the rock guitar band such as The Darkness; the public's voracious appetite for musical theatre (four new shows, *Mary Poppins*, *Billy Elliot*, *The Producers* and *The Woman in White* are set to open in the West End in the coming months), and the total dominance of the UK charts by AOR (Adult Orientated Rock) or easy-listening acts such as Dido and David Gray. Next year it could be something entirely different, so if you want to be a performer it pays to be flexible and to have a broad range of musical skills.

'Musicals are one of the identifying features of the West End Theatre, and since they are the biggest productions, playing in larger theatres with more personnel required than for straight drama, it follows that they must contribute significantly to the economics of the West End.'

Source: 'Counting The Notes'

THEIR BIG BREAK

Sometimes, just being in the right place at the right time can be the factor that turns a promising young performer into a real success story. Here is how four new stars got their big breaks:

- Devonshire teen Joss Stone was first noticed when she appeared on BBC TV's *Star for a night*. Since then she has recorded her critically acclaimed debut album 'The Soul Sessions' at Florida's famous TK studios, and can now count Tom Cruise as one of her biggest fans.

- Jazz-inspired pianist and vocalist Jamie Cullum became the subject of a bidding war after he sang on Michael Parkinson's Saturday night TV show in 2003. Universal eventually signed him for a £1 million deal.

- Nineteen-year-old Katie Melua is the protégée of veteran producer Mike Batt. Melua attended the Brit School for Performing Arts in Croydon where she studied a BTEC and a music A-level. Her debut album 'Call Off the Search' was championed by Radio 2 and knocked Dido's 'Life For Rent' off the top spot in the UK charts.

- Sixteen-year-old Erin Rocha was doing work experience at a Hampshire studio when she was asked if she could sing on a demo for a song called 'Can't do Right For Doing Wrong', a song intended for Nora Jones. Erin's version made it onto the A-playlist at BBC Radio 2 and she has subsequently been signed by EMI.

ADMINISTRATION/PRODUCTION

WRITERS AND COMPOSERS

No musical performer could do their job without the composers, lyricists and librettists who write the material they perform. In fact, in popular music many performers are actually singer/songwriters using their own material. However, some songwriters don't wish to perform themselves and write exclusively for other people. Some work in songwriting pairs where one person writes the music and the other person writes the lyrics. Famous songwriting pairs include Gilbert and Sullivan (light opera), Elton John and Bernie Taupin (pop), and Andrew Lloyd Webber and Tim Rice (musical theatre). If you are writing for the popular market you must take into account musical trends and fads, otherwise your songs will not sell. In fact, the singles market, at one time a lucrative area for songwriters, is currently in freefall and many radio stations now play album tracks rather than singles.

'The overall singles market decreased by 11.1 per cent in value in 2002. Spending on music isn't just influenced by the music industry – the explosion of DVD movie sales, the consolidation of mobile penetration and sliding economy all contribute to the contraction of consumer music spending.'

Source: British Phonographic Industry (BPI)
Annual sales figures report, 2002

PRODUCTION

Also close to the heart of the music making process is the producer. He or she works in the recording studio at the mixing desk and is responsible for the sound of the finished songs or musical piece. He or she will add effects, increase the bass, or soften the vocals in order to get the perfect mix. A good producer works incredibly closely with the musicians and singers and needs to have great empathy with them, coaxing out the best performances and suggesting different sounds or styles that will give their material that unique edge. Many producers are also musicians themselves, although some come up through being studio engineers learning the art of production on the job. Many pop acts become so attached to their producers they use them for all their recorded work.

MANAGEMENT

Just as important – and feared by many – is the all-powerful music manager. Anyone watching Simon Cowell demolish a would-be performer on *Pop Idol* will know managers speak their minds. They have to – it's their job. They are there to get the best deals for their acts, the most coverage in the media and to secure the best venues for them to play. They will liaise with the band or solo artist, with music companies and music publishers as well as organise tours, gigs, video shoots and TV appearances. For many the manager is God and for their troubles they will take a percentage of your earnings from records, tours and other promotional appearances.

'Managers such as Simon Fuller (Spice Girls and S Club 7) play an important role in shaping and developing their clients' careers . . . Professional managers are often the interface between the artist and record companies, music publishers, tour promoters, merchandisers and professional advisor, and they can command gross commission rates typically of 15 per cent and 20 per cent of artists' earnings.'

Source: 'Counting The Notes'

PUBLISHING COMPANY

Talking of money, the publisher or publishing company is a really important part of a musician's team. This is because they make sure you get all the monies you are owed for your songs and music. This happens in two ways. Firstly, you earn money from your music every time it is played on the TV or on the radio, in shopping malls or in lifts. A body called the Performing Rights Society (PRS) is responsible for collecting this money. Secondly, you also earn money from every CD, DVD and record that you sell. This money is collected by the Mechanical Copyright Protection Society (MCPS). The publisher will make sure all this money comes back to you. Some artists get publishing deals before they get a recording contract and the publisher will help them get media exposure.

DIRECTOR

In musical theatre the musical director does roughly the same job as a conductor in classical music, however his or her remit tends to be broader. They will take charge in the orchestra pit and also play an instrument (normally keyboards). They are responsible for rehearsals and sorting out any problems, so need to be at the theatre for considerable periods of time and not just for the performances.

BACKSTAGE/TECHNICIAN

Mounting any type of musical production, be it a rock concert tour, an opera at Glyndebourne, a video shoot, TV appearance, or classical show, involves the work of a lot of people you will never see, but whose absence you would notice if they weren't doing their jobs.

In theatres, stage managers are the logisticians, ensuring everything is where it should be, sourcing props and making sure the production doesn't go over budget. The lighting technicians are responsible for both designing and rigging the lights, which can be extremely sophisticated, while the sound technicians are responsible for the microphones, the amplifiers and the mixing desk, ensuring the perfect quality of the sound. Most large bands these days also have instrument technicians who make sure the guitars, keyboards and drums are all in tune and undamaged. Meanwhile, the roadies are responsible for the safe arrival, repackage and transport of all the technical gear – including the lighting and sound equipment and any props being used. Other people that are essential to opera and musical theatre are set designers, make-up and hair departments, costume designers and wardrobe staff.

In the recording studio, the manager is responsible for getting acts into the studio and using the facilities, so they need good contacts with record companies and also with agents. They may be responsible for the bookings system and will certainly coordinate the studio staff, the producers and the bands, and make sure the studio or studios have the most up-to-date equipment that is in good working order. Engineers need a lot of technical knowledge because they have to make certain everything is running smoothly, from the microphones to the mixing desk and recording equipment. Studio time can be enormously expensive so acts need to know they are not going to arrive and discover a problem. Engineers may employ the help of assistant engineers and tape operatives (ops).

SUPPORT STAFF

At the big record companies, a number of people are responsible for the well-being of their artists. These include the label manager who will sort out what type of budget is to be spent on each group and will help groom each act for success; the A&R (Artist and Repertoire) people who scout for new acts and hire them, then advise them on their career direction and progression; and the press officers responsible for sending out press releases, demo copies of records, arranging interviews on TV, radio and in newspapers and magazines, and accompanying their artists when they make public appearances.

Some of the more successful artists may have their own stylists who choose their clothes for them to wear on stage, in videos and at award ceremonies, and arrange to 'borrow' outfits from designers for them to wear.

Voice coaches and music teachers are a vital part of the music industry, as you should never stop learning. The majority of music teachers are classically trained. If you want to teach music at a state school you need to become a qualified teacher. If you are a graduate you can achieve this by taking a one-year PGCE. If you want to concentrate on singing coaching or the teaching of a specific instrument, you can take a teaching or a performance diploma.

RELATED ROLES

If you really want to work in the music business but have no musical skills you could always work for a ticket office or ticket agent such as Ticketmaster. You could work on merchandising, selling the T-shirts, posters and baseball caps of famous artists to their fans. Some people become promoters, booking venues and selling tickets to concerts. Others become radio DJs, TV presenters, public relations managers and music journalists, simply because they love music, even if they can't make it as a performer.

TANIA PEACH, 32, PRODUCTION MANAGER, MOUNTVIEW THEATRE ACADEMY

Tania took Technical Theatre at Rose Bruford College but left early when she was offered a job with a company specialising in outdoor trapeze and theatre and toured extensively in Europe with them. She also worked with Oxfordshire Touring and Paynes Plough before joining Mountview in 2003. Tania is doing an MA in Arts Administration and Cultural Policies with a view to going into general and venue management.

'Here at Mountview we do approximately 16 productions a year and it's a pretty hectic schedule. I have to oversee the freelancers we bring in to work on the shows as well as the students who staff the shows. I have to coordinate the scheduling, the budgeting for the staff, and the production budget for the show. I do a lot of venue liaison and even though I don't generate the contracts I operate the contracts with the venues making sure their staff don't go into overtime. There is a lot of logistics in terms of van movements, people movements, and equipment movements. Creatively I work quite closely with the directors and the designers before they even go into rehearsals. We look at the parameters and see how we can make the design work in the space available. I'm basically responsible for the practical input of the design.

'The two performance courses I deal with the most are the undergraduate acting course and the musical theatre course. We do a cross-section of shows, from Shakespeare to Brecht, to fairly large-scale musicals, which is why we tend to go to outside venues because they have better facilities for flying, etc, than we do here. One of the most important skills I bring to my job is being able to see the big picture, the overview, and another is people management. You definitely need communication skills too.

'Another important skill is being able to marry artistic ideas with practicalities and budgets. I used to think of the financial aspect of the job as a necessary evil, but now I quite enjoy it, I actually find it quite creative. A grasp of the financial side is essential because you work quite a lot with spreadsheets and Excel and you have to stay on top of it.

'Some of the worst things about the job are that you work very long, antisocial hours on fairly low budgets and so you are trying to perform miracles half of the time. There are times when the artistic side just won't marry with the practical side.

'I've always believed strongly in the creative element of the technician's role and how one collaborates and on what level. You are facilitating the work of the creatives and yet quite often your decisions as a technician inform the actual work. It is all interactive.

'The technical courses at Mountview really are like being in the industry, this is as close to the industry standard as you could possibly get, so if a student can do this they will be able to go straight out and get jobs in the industry. All the tutors are encouraged to keep abreast of what is going on as far as industry practice and contacts are concerned, because contacts are so important and we will get students work if we possibly can.'

CHRIS MARTIN, 22, 2ND YEAR TECHNICAL THEATRE DEGREE STUDENT SPECIALISING IN LIGHTING DESIGN
Chris has always been interested in drama and after doing Drama GCSE he started working front of house at a theatre. Part of the job involved frequent meetings with the backstage technicians and he liked what they did so much he too started working backstage. Through his work experience Chris received a scholarship to Mountview Theatre Academy.

'I do love performing but I want this job as a career and acting is so unpredictable so I decided to take up technical and keep acting as my hobby. As much as I love the theatre I am actually looking for work outside that field, so I'm exploring doing lighting for concerts, gigs and big clubs. In fact, I'm off to Israel as soon as I finish at Mountview to work as the Head of Lighting for a big sound company. They hire out equipment for hotels and events such as discos, concerts and corporate events.

'I think the best thing about what I do is the sense of achievement you get after a show. To have your lighting design viewed on stage or set and to have someone say your lights were good is a great thrill. For my job you need to be really creative and you have to have an eye for design, vision and a strong imagination. With lighting design it is all trial and error. You can draw something up but you won't know what it looks like until you've actually tried it out on set. You really have to understand what you are working with and what you are working towards.

'These days when you do a show the technical staff get the same respect for what they are doing as the actual performers because let's face it, they wouldn't be able to do the show without you. More and more, people are appreciating the backstage input into shows, especially as they get more technically complex and spectacular.

'I can't really think of any downsides to the industry, although the financial side is not that good when you first start out. A lighting technician straight from college will probably only earn between £13,000 and £16,000, however you can earn substantial sums as you get more experienced. Sometimes big egos can cause a problem but in the theatre industry there is very little leeway for mistakes and that makes people sort out their problems very quickly. Here at Mountview they drum into us that we are working as a company and they teach us how to deal with ego problems and control them.

'Ultimately, I'd like to be a lighting consultant and a touring designer. I'd like to be the person people come to and say, "what can we do about this?" I want to do big events. I'm planning to take a one-year City & Guilds qualification in electronics because I know that will help with my understanding of the equipment.

'My advice to anyone thinking about doing this as a career is go and see shows because you need to understand the basics. Get involved: get a job in front of house at your local theatre; join an amateur dramatic society; volunteer to help out backstage. All of those experiences will really help you.'

MARINA HADJIPANAYI, 21, 2ND YEAR TECHNICAL THEATRE DEGREE STUDENT SPECIALISING IN STAGE MANAGEMENT

'At school I did drama and dance and did some shows. It was there I saw people working backstage and decided rather than go through the pressure associated with being an actor or dancer I would prefer to be backstage myself. I got GCSEs in Drama, Music, English, Science, Maths and Design Communications, and when I was looking for degree courses I decided I'd like to specialise in Stage Management because it means you are involved in everything that is going on.

'A stage manager has to be very good at organisation and at communication, and must be able to stay on top of everything all the time. I think being organised is definitely the most important. Because your job is all about telling other people what to do you need to be able to show your authority but without offending people too much. The best thing about it is to watch everything come together under your control, and if things aren't working smoothly it's great to find ways to work round it so that it does.

'The thing with this job is that it does take up a lot of your time – it becomes your life. You spend hours and hours at the theatre and then you find you take your job home with you as well. It is very demanding, so don't think this is an easy job to get into. The antisocial hours can be a big turn off, especially if you are not enjoying the show you are doing. However, if you have a good team you find that you socialise with them and spend time with them outside of work hours and that's great.

'I don't mind where I work after I graduate. I just want to have the experience of being in the real world and seeing how it works. Later on, I wouldn't mind going into teaching stage management because I think it would give me a great sense of achievement to teach someone else what I have learned.'

Singing for Your Supper

As with all the other performing arts, a job for life in music may be hard to come by. This is why nearly every musician and singer will have skills that make it possible for them to find alternative employment when the musical pickings are slim. The only good thing about working in the evenings is that it leaves your days free to earn money by teaching or doing session work. Some people can and do make an awful lot of money from music, as illustrated in the box below, but you should not bet on that happening to you.

WHAT WILL YOU EARN?

The Musicians' Union set basic pay rates for musicians and you may be surprised at how modest they are (the figures quoted here are a guideline only). The minimum for a musician in an armed forces band is around £10,000, while members of orchestras earn from £13,500. If you are working freelance you may get £30 for a two-hour gig while freelance classical musicians may get £70 per concert. Obviously, rates within the West End tend to be higher. A musician in the pit for a West End show earns around £800 per week, while an Assistant Musical Director earns about £850 weekly and a Musical Director between £1000 and £1500 when doing eight shows a week. This works out at approximately 20 hours of playing time, as well as all the other work you do on top.

Positions in the West End are fiercely competitive because there are so few seats available (*Miss Saigon* employed 27 musicians, *Oliver!* 25 and *Chitty Chitty Bang Bang* just 19). The same is true in opera as there are so few jobs available. For instance, in 2000, according to the Arts Council of England, just 556 artistic staff were employed on a permanent basis in major opera companies in the country, while 1010 artistic staff were employed on a contract or freelance basis.

WE'RE IN THE MONEY
EARNINGS OF THE TEN WEALTHIEST BRITISH ACTS IN 2003

1. The Rolling Stones (£55.3 million)

2. Sir Paul McCartney (£40 million)

3. Sir Elton John (£34 million)

4. Robbie Williams (£30 million)

5. Coldplay (£25.3 million)

6. Sting (£25.14 million)

7. Phil Collins (£25.12 million)

8. Fleetwood Mac (£23.5 million)

9. Iron Maiden (£17.9 million)

10. Dido (£15.8 million)

Source: *Heat* magazine. Based on record sales, DVDs, touring, royalties, merchandising and other income

---

SCHOOL OF ROCK

If you have really decided that a career in music is for you then, as a performer, there are some things you should already be doing.

- If you want to be a musician you should be playing at least one instrument in the school band or orchestra (if there is one) and taking graded examinations.

- If you want to be a singer you should already be in your school choir or choral group (if there is one) and taking lessons and graded examinations.

- If possible, enter competitions such as the BBC's 'Young Musician of the Year'.

- There may well be an amateur operatic company in your area that could do with some help. Offer your services. The same is true if your local amateur dramatic society does musical productions.

- Some music colleges, like the Royal College of Music (RCM), offer opportunities and training to gifted students up to the age of 18. The RCM's Junior Department operates on Saturdays only and is an intense and very high quality course of study, training and worskshops. Only extremely talented students are accepted and there may be financial assistance for successful candidates.

- Above all you must **practise**. This is a career where dedication, energy, focus and hard work will really pay dividends.

Metier and Skillseekers can offer advice on S/NVQs and Modern Apprenticeships within the world of music (Edexcel has a number of courses it approves including a BTEC First Diploma in Performing Arts (Music) and both a National Certificate and a National Diploma in Performing Arts (Musical Theatre); see Resources). These will all be extremely useful if you decide to take a degree in music where you will also normally need two A-levels (including Music) as entrance requirements (for classical music courses you also need Grade 8 on your first instrument and Grade 5 on your second). The Foundation Modern Apprenticeship Schemes in arts and entertainment developed by Metier in England and Wales tend to be more on the practical side (working in a studio or backstage) where the apprentice receives training on the job while earning a wage. Normally, training is up to

S/NVQ Level 3 and is only open to people between 16 and 24 years old. If you are interested in a Modern Apprenticeship contact your local Learning and Skills Council (LSC) in England and Wales, or Local Enterprise Council (LEC) in Scotland (see Resources).

If you are seriously considering taking a music degree do bear in mind that of the 2,150 students who graduated in music in 2002, around 750 continued in further study or training (about 35 per cent) rather than going straight into employment. Of these one third took teacher training courses, either in the shape of the PGCE (necessary if you want to teach in a state school), or teaching or performance diplomas if they wanted to teach singing or an instrument in the private sector. (Source: HESA.) Other postgraduate courses include PhDs in Music Technology, Musical Composition, and Musicology, as well as MAs in Advanced Musical Studies, and in Music Therapy (see box below).

BRITISH SOCIETY FOR MUSIC THERAPY

A music therapist works with people who find it difficult to communicate verbally. Using instruments as well as the voice the therapist helps these people – either in a group or individually – to find their own 'voice' through music.

For more details, contact the British Society for Music Therapy, which publishes both the *British Journal of Music Therapy* and the *BSMT Bulletin*.
BSMT
61 Church Hill Road
East Barnet
Herts EN4 8SY
Tel: 020 8441 6226
Website: www.bsmt.org

LOST IN MUSIC

DECIDING WHAT TO STUDY

Which degree course you take will be entirely dependent on where your interests lie. What you must decide is how much of the course you take should be on the practical side and how much on the theoretical side. If your intention is to sing and/or play once you have graduated, then you should opt for a course where a high percentage of your time is spent on instrument or vocal tuition (it pays to find out the names of the professional musicians the college or university employs to teach you). Example degree titles include Professional Musical Theatre National Diploma, Music Composition and Professional Practice, BMus (Hons) Jazz, and BMus (Hons) Music.

You should be aware that because the teaching on these courses is on an intense, often one-to-one basis, you may have to pay for it yourself and so you need to take account of this in your budget. If you are looking to do something other than perform after graduation, an onus on theory might suit you better. Here, the subjects you can study become so diverse almost all interests can be covered. For example you can study Music and Comparative Literature, Music and Psychology, and even Music and Sport Studies. This is why it pays to send off for information and prospectuses early, so you can see what is out there. Where you go and what course you take will influence what it is you actually learn. Below are two examples of course programmes.

ON COURSE
At the Royal College of Music, the BMus (Hons) undergraduate programme aims to create professional musicians.

Key Features:

- Study on an instrument related to your Principal Study (e.g. cor anglais (English Horn) alongside oboe)

- Ensemble activities include chamber music coaching by specialist professors

- Units in professional skills to prepare you for the realities of the music profession (financial, concert and career planning)

- Units in historical, technical and practical subjects including communication and problem solving

● The course offers exchange opportunities with leading international conservatories including Juilliard and Year 3 and 4 students often study in Europe for a term.

Source: The Royal College Of Music (RCM)

ON COURSE

At the Mountview Theatre Academy you can study for the three-year BA (Hons) in Performance with a Musical Theatre option.

Key Features:

● The opportunity to explore and develop a career in performance in theatre and television, pop, cabaret and session work

● Students are taught to combine acting, singing and movement in their presentation of a seamless journey of character

● Within the course equal emphasis is given to the disciplines of singing, dance, movement, voice and acting

● All students have weekly, one-to-one singing lessons and regular vocal coaching sessions

● Year 2 students are taught the skills to devise and write a musical

● Year 3 students concentrate on public performances at Mountview's own venues and other London theatres

● In their final term, students present a West End showcase attended by agents, casting directors and members of the industry.

Source: Mountview Academy of Theatre Arts

LESS TRADITIONAL OPTIONS

Increasingly, students are looking for colleges where they can study contemporary music, and the jobs surrounding it, in a contemporary setting. Attracting a lot of attention is the BRIT School for Performing Arts & Technology in Croydon. Established 12 years ago and jointly funded by the government and the British Record Industry Trust, it has a state-of-the-art studio, theatre and even its own radio station. The emphasis here is on vocational work and it is the only performing arts school in Britain where entry is free for students between the ages of 14 and 19 years. However, competition for places is fiercer here than almost anywhere else due to the success of former students such as Amy Winehouse and Katie Melua. Each year only 130 14-year-olds and 300 to 350 16-year-olds are taken on and there are often three to four applicants for every place. Selection is based on audition, workshops and interviews and only the most talented get accepted. For more information see Resources.

In Brighton there is the Brighton Institute of Modern Music (BIMM) that opened in 2002 and now has about 350 students spread across its courses. Here, students study guitar, bass, drums or vocals at three levels: Diploma in Modern Music (equivalent to A-level), Higher Diploma (equivalent to first year of a degree course) and a BA in Professional Musicianship (Diploma and Higher Diploma are accredited by Edexcel, the BA by Sussex University). The emphasis is on performance and on learning about the profession, so all students get the chance to attend masterclasses with the likes of Feeder, Motorhead, and Skunk Anansie, while many get to play with name bands while still at the institute (students have appeared on *Top Of The Pops* and have done live shows with the likes of Atomic Kitten and The Sugababes). For more information see Resources.

FASCINATING FACT

Impala (Independent Music Publishers' and Labels' Association) represents more than 2,000 independent (indie) labels across Europe and has filed a petition against a merger between industry giants Sony Music and BMG. Impala claims the £3.4 billion merger would take a

quarter of all music sales and squeeze out sales by indies
who do not have huge marketing budgets to advertise
their artists. In the UK, 700 smaller labels account for up
to 25 per cent of the UK retail market while the 'big 5' –
Universal, Sony, EMI, Warner and BMG – control 74 per
cent of the world market.

Source: Impala

MONEY'S TOO TIGHT TO MENTION

FUNDING YOUR TRAINING

As stated previously in the Drama section of this book, at present,
students entering higher education in the state system pay an
upfront student fee contribution of £1,125 per year towards the
cost of their course. Under proposed new government policy this
is to rise to up to £3,000 per year in 2006 (to be paid on
graduation). However, students from lower-income backgrounds
can apply for help with this fee and can also apply for student
loans to cover living costs (at present the maximum loan is
£4,000). For more information on Higher Education funding, the
DfES publishes a guide, *Financial Support For Higher Education
Students*, which is available from the DfES Information Line on
0800 731 9133. For more information on the DfES, see Resources.

Extremely talented young musicians between the ages of 8 and 18
may be able to get a scholarship under the Music and Dance
Scheme (MDS) run by the DfES. This allows them to continue
their academic education while getting the best possible music
training available. For more information contact the DfES.

Non-UCAS (Universities and Colleges Admissions Service) and
private schools and colleges can be very expensive (for example,
Arts Educational Schools London has a three-year National
Diploma in Professional Music Theatre that costs £8,205) but, as
in drama, many music colleges and schools offer bursaries and
scholarships to the most talented students and you may be able
to get sponsorship for your studies. (Full information on how to
obtain sponsorship or scholarships is contained in the Funding
your Studies section of Chapter 4, Courses for Horses.)

FASCINATING FACT

Actor Kelsey Grammer, best known for being TV's *Frasier*, is so enamoured of ITV's *The Sketch Show* that he has made his own version for the American market. The show, shot at London's Teddington Studios, stars British comic Lee Mack alongside a host of American TV stars with Grammer as guest star and executive producer.

I Could Have Danced All Night

DANCING UNCOVERED

Watching the professional dancer plying his or her trade is a visual treat we can all enjoy, be it Darcey Bussell performing classical ballet at the Royal Opera House or young Jamie Bell showing off his more contemporary moves in the film *Billy Elliot*. In fact, the variety of different styles is much wider than you might think and in recent years the world of dance has really opened up with successful shows such as *Tap Dogs* and *Riverdance* bringing dance to a wider audience. Although dance breaks down into three main areas (classical dance, contemporary dance and musical theatre) the range of styles includes ballet, tap, jazz, South Asian, flamenco, tango, salsa, ballroom, African and even break-dancing. You can see dancers in films and theatre shows such as *Chicago* and *Cabaret*, in music videos, in clubs, restaurants and hotels and at large corporate extravaganzas, exhibitions and displays, some even work in the circus such as the performers in Cirque Du Soleil.

FASCINATING FACT

In 2002 there were 2300 dance and drama graduates. Approximately 71 per cent went straight into employment with around 46 per cent gaining full-time paid work. 16 per cent opted to take further studies.

Source: HESA

I'M IN THE MOOD FOR DANCING

DO YOU HAVE WHAT IT TAKES?

Not everyone who wants to be a dancer has the necessary skills or physical attributes to make it. Ballet, in particular, requires girls to be between 1.52 metres and 1.67 metres tall, while boys must be between 1.6 metres and 1.78 metres tall. Other dance forms have less stringent physical requirements, but you will still need grace and rhythm and the ability to communicate with an audience through movement to enjoy a successful career. If you don't have the natural skills and talent to be a professional dancer yourself but desperately want to work within the dance sphere, do not despair, there are plenty of other jobs you can do, some of which you might not even know about. Most of these will be in the backstage area and include make-up artists, the wardrobe department and technical crews responsible for the sound and lighting of shows. You could be a dance journalist or photographer or a therapist, such as an osteopath, who specialises in dance injuries. The chart below will show you just some of the occupations available to people who want to work in the dance world.

BEST FOOT FORWARD

As you've probably realised by now, making it as a professional dancer is tough. Because it takes years of physical conditioning if you haven't actually started training in any form of dance by your mid-teens, it is probably too late to consider becoming a performer seriously. However, if you are already some way along the dancing ladder there are some physical and mental abilities and skills that are really going to help you.

JOBS IN DANCE

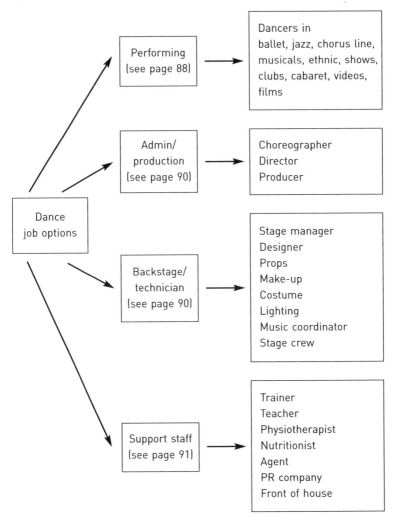

GOOD HEALTH

Dancers are like athletes in that they use their bodies as the tools of their trade. This means they cannot afford ill health and must constantly look after themselves and monitor their fitness. Also, in the same way in which athletes employ the services of sports physiotherapists and trainers, so too do dancers. Many dancers do yoga and Pilates for body conditioning and regularly visit masseuses, physiotherapists, osteopaths and chiropractors. A dancer's body is like an expensive car – it needs to be finely tuned at all times.

STAMINA

Although actual performances (or a particular dancer's role in them) may only last a few minutes or a couple of hours this is not the end of the physical story. Dancers have to be constantly at their physical peak. This means they will have regular practice sessions. And the story doesn't end there because they will also have frequent rehearsals for performances. They may be aching from the exertions of the day before, but they still have to put in those hours at the dance studio. It can be physically exhausting and dancers must constantly watch their stamina levels.

DETERMINATION

It may be very early in the morning and freezing outside but the show has to go on which means dancers have still got to rehearse. Endlessly repeating the same sequence of movements for a particular piece may seem mind-numbingly boring but any dancer worth his or her salt will be determined to get it right, not just because customers pay good money to watch performances, but because if you are performing in an ensemble one dancer's mistake could throw out the performances of everyone else on stage.

FASCINATING FACT

The morning of the film shoot for the famous dance scene in *Singin' in the Rain*, star Gene Kelly woke up with a raging fever and a cold. Being the perfectionist he was, he insisted on completing the shoot, even though it meant dancing in a downpour of rain. The result is one of the most shown clips in film history.

ATTENTION TO DETAIL

Although as a spectator you may not always see the complexity and precision of every movement on stage, the dancer most definitely does. He or she will know when a hand is at the wrong angle, or a foot is in the wrong place, and the best dancers are those who are not satisfied with nearly right, but with perfection. This constant need to be better at what they do marks out really good dancers from the mediocre (see Celia Grannum's case study).

GOOD SPATIAL MEMORY

Your spatial memory helps you remember where your arm or leg is in relation to the space around you. Dancers use their spatial memories to learn their dance steps, so they can remember how high they should hold their arms and which movement follows which within a dance piece. Dancers memorising choreography is a bit like actors learning their lines, except for the dancer the whole body is involved. If you have a good spatial memory it will help you to learn new routines quickly, ensuring that rehearsals go much more smoothly.

CONCENTRATION

Closely aligned to spatial memory is concentration, because the harder you concentrate on what you are doing, the more quickly you can master it. Some dance pieces may not be very long, but they can contain hundreds of precise movements, some of which have to be executed at speed, so if you don't concentrate you could end up in a knotted pile in the corner. You have to sustain your concentration until the end of the piece and this is even more important when dancing as part of a corps de ballet or in a chorus line where lots of people are on stage at the same time. If you end up facing the wrong way in the wrong place, you can put out the placements for the whole of the group. If you are a male dancer lifting a dancing partner concentration is crucial because one slip could lead to a serious injury.

PASSION

It may sound corny, but you really do need a passion for what you do to make it in dance. This is because there will always be someone out there hungrier, who wants it more than you, and when it comes to getting jobs it is the hungry dancer who gets the fattest worms! Dancing jobs are at a premium and no one wants to watch a mediocre dancer who can't really be bothered to put in the effort. A passionate dancer will receive the best job offers and the biggest accolades each and every time.

ALL THAT JAZZ

ARE YOU BUILT TO DANCE?

If all of the above are going to help you make it in the world of dance, then there are some mental and physical attributes that could seriously hold you back. Check the list below to see whether a career in dancing is a viable option for you.

PHYSICAL PROBLEMS

Most of us would love to imagine ourselves moving effortlessly and gracefully along to a musical rhythm; unfortunately for many it remains a dream as they seem to have been born with two left feet. If you suffer from a lack of coordination or from extreme clumsiness (known as dyspraxia) mastering complex dance moves is going to be difficult. If you have a physical disability, opportunities to work within the dance arena will be limited, although some dance troupes have actually turned this into their own unique selling point. CandoCo is a contemporary dance group that contains both able-bodied and disabled dancers and runs training courses for the disabled (for more details see Resources). Physical problems obviously include injuries, many of which are caused by dancers lifting other dancers. This is why the most common injuries in men involve back problems, while in female dancers it is the hips that suffer the most. The most common physical problem of all though is arthritis, where the joints become inflamed because of overuse and overstretching. Such problems can shorten a dancer's career quite considerably.

FASCINATING FACT

During the teen years both boys and girls put on a growth spurt. This distorts the body's own spatial memory of itself and it takes a little while to get used to having longer legs and arms. This leaves many teenagers permanently tired (from all that growing) and extremely clumsy and accident-prone. During this time certain dance exercises they could once perform easily become almost impossible for them. However, once the spurt slows down and the body 'recognises' its new size they soon find their old physical prowess returning.

CAREER LONGEVITY

A dancing career is almost certainly not going to last you for life, so you will have to come to terms with the fact that your days on stage are numbered. Most dancers accept this and make provision for life after dancing by establishing themselves as a dance teacher or by having another skill, such as becoming a physical therapist of some sort (yoga or Pilates teacher/physical conditioning practitioner/nutritionist). However, if the thought of having to change careers while friends outside the industry are just beginning to establish themselves in theirs fills you with dread, maybe you should consider one of the alternatives as your main career from the outset.

HEIGHT

Ideas about the way dancers should look may be slowly (ever so slowly) changing, but there is a good reason why dancers (especially ballet dancers) have traditionally been of modest height. It's because when dancing duets they will frequently be lifted by their partner and the smaller you are the easier you are to lift. There is also an aesthetic aspect to it, because the visual contrast of a muscular male dancer with his petite female partner is seen as very pleasing. Many companies want the dancers in their corps de ballet or chorus line to be the same height because it gives visual symmetry when they are on stage. If you are tall your height may count against you. However, more contemporary or non-western dance may suit you better. In fact, the famous Bluebell Girls from Paris's Moulin Rouge (home of the cancan) all have to be over six foot in height!

WEIGHT

Dancers and their weight is a very serious issue. If you are overweight you may find it difficult to compete in the job market against other dancers with slimmer figures. Once again, if a male dancer is going to be lifting you, then the smaller you are the easier his job becomes. However, the obsession with body shape and size within the dance community is one the industry itself is addressing. This is because so many dancers suffer from eating disorders. Sad to say, but there are still some dance companies where dancers are encouraged to be as skinny as possible. In order to get skinny and stay skinny some dancers will starve themselves, leading to all sorts of physical problems both in the short and long term. Dance UK is the national development agency for dance and is well aware of the situation. In response it has produced the Healthier Dance Programme giving advice on health and nutrition (see Resources for more information).

ATTENTION DEFICIT/LACK OF DISCIPLINE

If your mind keeps wandering off the job in hand you are never going to make it as a dancer where pinpoint timing is sometimes the only thing between you and crashing into the audience. Non-stop practice trains your body to follow the choreography but it is up to you to keep your mind on track. You have to be disciplined, not just about the dancing practice but also about your diet and lifestyle – if you have an important performance coming up you can't afford to spend hours partying with friends. If you think you may lack the discipline to be tucked up in bed early while others are out enjoying themselves, you may have to think again about a career in dance.

SUSCEPTIBILITY TO STRESS

Some people find they really can't hack it as dancers because they just cannot cope with performance stress.'Stage fright' can afflict the most seasoned professional but most find some kind of coping mechanism (which is why so many of them practise yoga or meditation). If you are simply paralysed by nerves each and every time you go to dance in front of an audience, you may like to consider some other job within the dance area otherwise you could end up with a serious stress-related illness.

ANTISOCIAL HOURS

As in the worlds of drama and music, most dance performances will take place in the evenings and at weekends when the audience can get away from its own work. This means dancers may spend many hours in rehearsal or at dance class during the day and then find themselves working on stage at night. You may also go off on tour with your dance company meaning your hours become even more irregular (think of the travel involved). Not only the performers work antisocial hours, but also the technical people involved in putting on dance shows. If you are looking for a cosy 9 to 5 you may like to consider other areas of employment in the industry.

FASCINATING FACT

Proving the exception to the rule, the great Russian ballet dancer Mikhail Baryshnikov is still performing in public at the age of 56. This year he appeared at the Barbican Theatre in London, dancing pieces by a number of choreographers including Britain's Michael Clark.

SPOTLIGHT ON RAMBERT DANCE COMPANY

- The Rambert Dance Company is Britain's oldest established dance company, dating back to 1926 when Frederick Ashton created his first ballet *A Tragedy Of Fashion*

- The Company was established by Polish-born Marie Rambert (1888–1982), who was inspired to dance having seen Isadora Duncan perform in Warsaw

- Marie Rambert's favourite discoveries were Frederick Ashton and Antony Tudor

- In 1966, modern dance training was added to its classical ballet training and the company still trains in the two styles

- The size of the company has ranged from 12 to 35 dancers and it now averages 22

- Ballet Rambert was the first British dance company to perform in China in 1958

- Audrey Hepburn, Vanessa Redgrave and Darcey Bussell all trained at the Ballet Rambert School

- In 2003, Rafael Bonachela choreographed '21' in which Kylie Minogue appeared in specially created projections.

Source: the Rambert Dance Company

Dancing Queens (and Kings)

'Dancing, for me, is almost a spiritual experience.'
Celia Grannum, freelance professional dancer

WHAT JOBS ARE THERE?

The chart on page 81 will have given you some idea of what career opportunities actually exist in dance and here we will explore what each job within the industry entails.

PERFORMING

The opportunities for dancers have increased dramatically in the last twenty years. For a start, more people than ever are taking dance classes – everything from ceroc to salsa – and this has increased their interest in seeing live dance as entertainment. Where once dance was viewed as being quite elitist, mainly because classical ballet was the only live dance form you could actually go to see and was horrendously expensive, new shows like *Lord of the Dance* and renewed interest in flamenco and tango have brought a new, younger and trendier audience to dance. This renewed interest means more dance shows, which means more dancers. Also, the dance club culture of the 1990s has increased dance's exposure on television, film and video.

In the 1970s, John Travolta became famous for his dance moves in *Saturday Night Fever*, which led to the explosion of the disco craze across the world. Dancing is still popular in films today, such as the Hollywood blockbusters *Chicago* and *Moulin Rouge*.

In 2004 the film *Honey*, starring Jessica Alba of TV's *Dark Angel*, was released in Britain. Alba plays a young New York dancer and choreographer who gets her big break choreographing the dance routines for music videos by the likes of Missy Elliott and Ginuwine. The film was directed by Bille Woodruff, who has directed videos for Britney Spears and Usher. Choreography was by Laurieann Gibson who has worked with P. Diddy, Mary J. Blige and Brandy.

Dancers now work for established dance companies like Rambert Dance Company and the Royal Ballet, they work as session dancers for TV shows and for videos, they work live on stage in musical theatre, they work in nightclubs and in cabaret, some even put on the floor shows in holiday camps and on cruise liners. Some specialise in classical ballet, others in one or more areas of contemporary dance, still others like Joaquin Cortes have only one speciality (flamenco).

THE LIFE OF A PERFORMER

A dancer's life is a demanding one, with hours of practice and rehearsals to get through as well as performance stress and the physical stress of demanding one hundred per cent from your body on a daily basis. They must watch out for injury and keep up to date with the latest dance trends and moves, which entails taking lots of dance classes. Many dancers go on tour and all that travelling can bring its own demands and problems.

Most dancers tend to be freelance and go from job to job and contract to contract and just like actors and musicians, dancers expect to spend some time out of work, that is why it is so important for them to have other skills they can use for alternative employment (many teach dance, more of which below).

ADMINISTRATION/PRODUCTION

Many dancers go on to do their own choreography; in fact many choreographers are very talented dancers in their own right (Britain's Michael Clark for one). The choreographer's job is to come up with the dance moves the dancers then follow – he or she is a bit like a musical composer, but they use movements instead of notes. You need a sound technical knowledge of dance for this job and for many dancers this is their preferred career route when they retire from active dancing themselves. While the choreographer concentrates on what the dancers are doing, the director of a dance show is intent on getting all the elements – lighting, dancing, costume, music – coming together and being right on the night (a bit like a conductor), while the producer has to make sure everything goes to budget and that the costs do not over-run astronomically.

Dance notation is the art of writing dance movements down, a bit like a composer notating music and, as in music, there are now specific computer software packages to make the task of notating easier. This is a pretty specialised job and you need to have a genuine passion for dance to have an interest in notating.

BACKSTAGE/TECHNICIAN

As in all areas where live performance or televised or filmed performance is concerned, the technical staff are essential. This becomes especially true with live dance, where safety concerns are paramount. Set designers must ensure their artistic visions don't endanger the dancers. No one wants to see the sugarplum fairy fall over a piece of scenery. Likewise, the costume designer must ensure the dancers can actually move in their outfits.

Although the Royal Ballet can mount very extravagant productions, many contemporary companies actually use very pared-down sets and costumes, but this is not true of all areas in dance. As we saw in the Drama section, musical theatre is hugely popular in Britain and although these are not pure dance shows many contain dance numbers. Audiences pay large sums to see the stunning visual effects and props in shows such as *Les Miserables*, *Chitty Chitty Bang Bang* and *Miss Saigon* and so the input of lighting and sound technicians, prop masters and special effects teams is invaluable. Other areas backstage you might like to consider are make-up, wig-maker and wardrobe.

SUPPORT STAFF

Like actors, many established dancers are members of Equity and have their own agents. He or she will inform their client about auditions and new shows coming up, and will generally promote their talents. Larger dance companies will have their own PR departments to liaise with TV and print journalists about forthcoming shows and guest star appearances. In fact, you could decide to become a dance journalist, reviewing live dance performances and reporting on dance news stories. One recent trend in dance has been the expansion of the community dance sector. The community dance worker may operate in conjunction with social services or the local education authority to help people of all ages and of all abilities to communicate through movement and dance.

The dance therapist has a similar role but will normally be working with people who have problems expressing their feelings and emotions through verbal communication. However, the most important members of support staff for a dancer are those that oversee their physical welfare. Many dancers become dance teachers whose role is not only vital for the education of young dancers coming into the system, but also to the established dancers who must keep practising on a daily basis.

Also essential are the physiotherapists, osteopaths, chiropractors and other physical therapists that help the dancer overcome injury and the physical stresses that dancing puts on the body. Many established companies employ their own physical therapists but most freelance dancers must pay for this themselves. Equity now offers dance members a special insurance scheme in case of injury.

FASCINATING FACT

The Critics' Circle National Dance Awards were founded in 1999 and they are the only professional awards in Britain dedicated specifically to the art of dance. Winners in the 2003 awards included an audience award for Adam Cooper, who also won the award for Best Choreography (Musical Theatre) for his show *On Your Toes*, Best Male Dancer award for Carlos Acosta of Royal Ballet, and Outstanding Female Artist (Modern) for Ana Lujan Sanchez of Rambert Dance Company.

Source: Critics' Circle, Dance Branch.
www.nationaldanceawards.com

**CELIA GRANNUM, 27, FREELANCE DANCER/
DANCE TEACHER/PILATES TEACHER**
Celia is originally from Barbados and trained at the TISCH School of the Arts, a part of New York University in America. When she first came to England she worked as a dance teacher at a boarding school in Surrey and is now involved with Exchange Music and Dance Company and Ballet Black.

'I've always had multiple interests and when you are freelancing you really need them because there will be times when you are not working. I still teach dance at the boarding school in Surrey and I also teach Pilates so that gives me a regular income. I have a friend who has done some dancing for a major pop star, and jobs like that are great because you get paid substantial sums and you can save them to tide you over during the lean times. I did a job for Iron Maiden last year for their single 'Rainmaker' where I had to wear a grass skirt and be covered in mud and be soaked all day and I got paid a measly £250 for that! But I love to dance. For me it is almost a spiritual experience. When I'm dancing it is almost as if I'm not here, I go somewhere else. It's the physicality of it, moving and feeling free in your body. It's a joy and an exhilaration and it's all about communicating with your audience.

'Injury is a serious consideration for anybody who is working with their body. At Ballet Black we get free physical therapy, but freelance dancers usually have to pay for it themselves and it can get very expensive. I have a recurring ankle injury and I am considering having an operation but I'm doing a lot of dance work at the moment so it's about finding the right time to do it.

'The other thing that is dangerous about dancing, apart from the physical, is the mental injury. If you do the more traditional styles of dance such as ballet you are always aiming for a physical ideal and you can get to a place in your head where you believe you are never good enough. If you keep telling yourself that every day then it becomes a self-fulfilling prophecy – you never will be good enough – and that wears away at your self-confidence. There's also the problem of weight. I've personally never had a weight problem but it can get to be so depending on whom you work for. Some companies do like their dancers to be extremely thin. You really have to watch out for that because it can make you paranoid and some dancers do end up starving themselves.

'I'd say to anyone out there considering this as a career to just follow their heart and don't be swayed. There are a lot of negatives attached to it but give it a shot and if it isn't for you then that's fine. Dancing is one of those things where you can't wait until later to get into it. So if you are 15 or 16 and have that burning desire to be a dancer try it out now because it is better to discover it's not working out now than to look back at the age of 40 and realise you can no longer give it a try because physically it's just too late.'

JOYCE AMBROSE, 24, PGCE TRAINEE DANCE TEACHER
Joyce studied for her BTEC National (equivalent to 2 A-levels) in Singing, Acting and Dancing and also did A-level Dancing before auditioning to Liverpool John Moores

University, to do a degree in Dance/Drama. As she is dyslexic, the university suggested she would do better just on the Dance course, which she subsequently did. She graduated in 2002 and took a year out to travel before starting her PGCE, also at John Moores.

'The degree course I did involved lots of dance in the community and the university said my social skills were so good that teaching would suit me as I wanted to work with people with disabilities and also with children. On the PGCE you have a teaching place three days a week in a school and two days in university and after half term in February this year, it will be five days a week in the school teaching just dance. You go into school as a dance specialist, basically you do your PGCE under PE with a lot of PE students, so my actual PGCE will say PE (Dance). I do hip hop, street dance, break-dancing, jazz, contemporary or modern but I don't really do that much ballet. I tend to do a lot of street dance in school to get the boys involved because they tend to think that dance is girlie – 'Boys don't do dance, dancing is for girls' – and I always ask them about break-dancing and teach them to do the caterpillar and the windmill.

'I do a lot of dance for myself as well. There's a place called Merseyside Dance Initiative in Liverpool and I do a lot of dance classes there because when you are a dance teacher it is very hard to actually get to do any dance yourself. You go in, warm up, show the class a routine, but you don't actually dance and from the performing side of it you get such a buzz. It's not that I don't get a buzz out of teaching, I leave after teaching on a high, but it is a very different feeling from performing. I do a contemporary class, a street-dance class and a break-dance class so I can see what's going on and what new moves are coming through. I don't always get to do them every week but I do as much as I can because it also helps me keep up with the music.

'Of course I would like to be a performer, but you look at what they have to be, they have to be a certain weight and a certain height and look a certain way and if you are not what they are looking for you get rejected and that can really hurt. I wouldn't want to put myself through that.

'I didn't start dancing until I was 15 when I went to a jazz class and when I got to university everyone had done ballet and I hadn't. So for six months I tried to teach myself as much as I could and I trained my body and I worked really hard because I believe you need to be passionate about what you are doing. Teaching dance may not be my first passion, dancing is, but it still has something to do with what I want to do and I know I'm good at it. You also have to be competitive – you can't help but judge yourself.

'You do need to have people skills to become a teacher. It's no good if you are timid in front of a class because the kids will suss you out. You also have to be authoritative and show them who's boss. You also need to know your subject, because they will always ask you the question you don't know the answer to! You can't expect your pupils to respect your subject if you don't respect it yourself. You will never ever be able to encourage other people to go on to do your subject. If you think dance has got value, and I do think it has, then your pupils will think it has value too. I do believe I am making a difference. I want to inspire my pupils.'

FASCINATING FACT

Beyonce Knowles appeared at the 2004 Brit Awards with an entourage of 20 dancers from LA. Unfortunately, the dancers' luggage went missing in transit and twenty pairs of silver ankle-strap shoes were hurriedly bought from Faith as replacements.

A World in Motion

'Be passionate about what you are doing because I think once you lose your passion, there is no point doing it. I still get excited about dancing, I really do.'
Joyce Ambrose, Trainee Dance Teacher

SHOW ME THE MONEY

Dancing with Beyonce may sound incredibly exciting, however it may not make you rich. Although it's true that big corporate affairs do tend to pay more than everyday dance events (they tend to have bigger budgets), they don't come along every week. In fact, most dancers, especially those in the corps de ballet or in the chorus line, get modest wages, it is only when you become a star or a known name that the money becomes substantial. Equity negotiates the minimum wages for dancers in the UK and for ballet and dance artists it is approximately £277 a week. A junior member of a corps de ballet earns between £14,000 and £17,500, while a soloist earns £22,000 and a principal £30,400. In contemporary dance the wages tend to be lower than in classical dance. Choreographers are paid slightly differently. In the West End they get a fee of approximately £2,524 for the work they have created and then an additional weekly payment of £506 while the piece is running. These fees are lower outside of the West End (approximately £907 and then £310).

TRANSFERABLE SKILLS
As in all areas of the performing arts, dancers can expect to have periods of unemployment and so should definitely acquire other skills. Many go into teaching (if you want to teach in a state school you will have to obtain a PGCE), especially as so many members of the public now take dance classes, and many study privately to become therapists in disciplines associated with keeping the body fit and healthy (masseuse, reflexologist, Pilates teacher). The one thing all dancers should bear in mind is that their performing career will be relatively short and so they should formulate a long-term career plan they are going to follow once their dancing days are over. Many go into arts administration, choreography and dance therapy.

DANCE CLASS

If you really believe you have what it takes to be a professional dancer then there are some things you should be doing already to increase your chances of success.

- If you have not started taking dance classes by your early teens you really need to start doing so **now**. This is especially true if you want to be a classical dancer. For ballet, girls need to start *at the very latest* by the age of 12, and boys by 14. You should be taking graded examinations (e.g. Royal Academy of Dancing, RAD). There are almost no opportunities for an adult in dance training.

- **Stay flexible**. This is true both physically and mentally. You need to keep yourself fit and healthy but you should also flex your mind by going to see as many dance performances as possible, in as many styles. Check out flamenco as well as ballet, street dance as well as contemporary.

- **Know your history**. If you can show a real love and knowledge of your subject it will give you an advantage over other candidates. There are plenty of books, videos and DVDs that will help you track the history of dance.

- **Practise!** Dance is a demanding discipline and if you start to let things slide it will show. They say 'practice makes perfect', and in dance the need to practise is paramount. If you don't have the passion and the motivation to practise regularly, you may like to consider doing something else within the dance arena.

- One of the best things you can do to show you really are committed to a career in dance is to take a vocational qualification such as a BTEC National Diploma or GNVQ (S/NVQ) in Performing Arts (Dance). Taken from the age of 16 this is a very popular way to prepare yourself for higher education in dance. Contact Metier and Skillset for more information (see Resources).

WHERE TO GO? WHAT TO DO?

Although academic qualifications are not mandatory, to get onto a dance course you will normally have to pass an audition (you may have to pay an audition fee of around £30), have an interview and in some cases a medical examination to assess your spatial awareness and physical articulation. Degree courses, however, normally have an entrance minimum of five GCSEs and two A-levels, or three Scottish Highers plus equivalent.

THE BIGGER PICTURE

Before applying for any course however, you should be thinking about what you want to do once you have finished training. If you want to enter the West End or do chorus-line work, a course at a musical theatre school where you train in a multitude of disciplines including acting, singing and jazz dance will be most appropriate. If contemporary dance is your forte then contemporary dance schools such as the London Contemporary Dance School offer thorough training in a variety of contemporary styles and techniques such as Cunningham or Graham, and usually include ballet as a main course subject. However, these courses are very expensive and places are much sought after.

Finally, if you are serious about becoming a ballet dancer, you should already be well into your training. The Music and Dance

Scheme (MDS) funds children and young people between the ages of 11 and 18 to receive an academic education alongside specialist music and ballet training. Four dance schools offer MDS places to students at 11: the Royal Ballet School, Elmhurst School For Dance and Performing Arts, The Hammond School, and Arts Educational School, Tring Park (for more information contact Council for Dance Education and Training (CDET), see Resources). Ballet training is very intensive and entry onto courses is strictly limited to those with exceptional skills and talent.

If you want to study dance on a more academic level, then a degree course at university might suit you. These will involve a certain amount of vocational training but will also cover theory, history, choreography and other subjects.

ON COURSE
A dance degree at university may include a number of the following topics:

- Directing

- Dance in the community

- Choreography

- Dance in education

- Mime/ballet

- Contemporary dance

- Performance

- History of dance

- Performance analysis.

Source: *CRAC Degree Course Guides 2003/4,
Music, Drama & Dance*, Trotman Publishing

However, if you really, really want to dance as a performer you should be looking for a place at a specialist dance school. Courses here tend to be of three years' duration. They usually lead to a degree or a diploma and will involve many hours each day in practical work. The Council for Dance Education and Training (CDET) accredits the following dance courses and they are inspected by government agencies as well as the CDET. All qualifications are awarded by Trinity College, London and you may be eligible for funding (see next section).

SCHOOL	COURSE/S	TYPE OF FUNDING
Arts Ed London	Musical Theatre Course 3 yr	DaDA
Arts Educational School Tring Park	Dance Course 2 yr	DaDA
Bird College	Dance & Theatre 3 yr	DaDA
	BA (Hons) Dance & Theatre 2 yr	DaDA
Central School of Ballet	Professional Performers 3 yr	DaDA
	Classical Ballet 2 yr	DaDA
Elmhurst	Classical Ballet & Contemporary 3 yr	DaDA
	Jazz Dance & Commercial Theatre 3 yr	DaDA
English National Ballet School	Intensive Classical Ballet Course 2 yr (not CDET accredited)	DaDA
The Hammond School	Dance Performance & Teaching 3 yr	DaDA
Italia Conti Academy	Performing Arts Course 3 yr	DaDA
Laban Centre	BA (Hons) Dance Theatre Course 3 yr	DaDA

SCHOOL	COURSE/S	TYPE OF FUNDING
Laban Centre cont.	Undergraduate Diploma Dance Theatre 3 yr	DaDA
	Professional Diploma 1 yr	DaDA
Laine Theatre Arts	Musical Theatre Performers 3 yr	DaDA
	& Teachers Course 3 yr	DaDA
Liverpool Theatre School	Musical Theatre Course 3 yr (not CDET accredited)	DaDA
London Contemporary Dance School	BA (Hons) Contemporary Dance 3 yr	HE state
	One year Certificate I yr	HE state
London Studio Centre	BA (Hons) Theatre Dance 3 yr	DaDA
	Diploma (HE) Theatre Dance 3 yr	DaDA
Merseyside Dance & Drama Centre	Teacher & Performance Course Dance 3 yr & Musical Theatre 3 yr	—
Midlands Academy of Dance & Drama	Musical Theatre Course 3 yr	—
Millennium Dance 2000	Professional Diploma in Performance 3 yr (not CDET accredited)	DaDA
Northern Ballet School	Professional Dancer's Course 3 yr	DaDA
	Dance Teacher's Diploma Course 3 yr	DaDA
Northern School Of Contemporary Dance	BPA Dance 3 yr	HE state
	National Diploma in Dance 3 yr (not CDET accredited)	HE state

SCHOOL	COURSE/S	TYPE OF FUNDING
Performers' College	Performers Theatre Dance course 3 yr	DaDA
Rambert School	BA (Hons) Ballet & Contemporary Dance 3 yr	HE state
Royal Ballet School	11 Plus Course 5 yr Dancer's Course 3 yr (not CDET accredited)	MDS MDS
Stella Mann College	Performers/Teachers Dance Course 3 yr	DaDA
SLP College	Teacher Training & Performing Arts Course 3 yr	—
Urdang Academy	Performers Course 3 yr	DaDA

Source: Council for Dance Education and Training

MONEY MATTERS

As previously mentioned, the Music and Dance Scheme (MDS) funds young people between the ages of 11 and 18 to train for a career in ballet. Funding is income related, so the amount received will depend on the income of parents or guardians. Contact the DfES for more information.

MAINTAINED OR STATE FUNDED

On these courses, students pay a student fee contribution (£1,125 per year) to the course fees but if you come from a low income background you can apply for help. You can also apply for a student loan for help in covering the cost of travel, accommodation etc. (at present the maximum amount of maintenance loan is £4,000). However, this is set to change in 2006 when the student fee contribution could rise to £3,000. For more information, contact the DfES information line: 0800 731 9133.

DANCE AND DRAMA AWARDS (DaDA)

Introduced in 1999, these awards help with fees and maintenance for talented students wishing to go into dance. Courses eligible for DaDA funding can be one, two or three years in duration. Your financial circumstances may be taken into account when an award is given, but this is only secondary to your talent. Only 60 per cent of students on a particular course will be provided with DaDAs, the rest will have to fund their own places.

FULL COST OR INDEPENDENT COURSES

Vocational training in dance does not come cheap; this is because classes are often small or the training is provided on a one-to-one basis. Courses that do not attract funding from the state sector can cost upwards of £10,000 per year. However, you may still be able to find financial help in the form of a scholarship or bursary. Many dance schools have funds specifically aimed at talented students who need help in covering course fees. For these you must enquire direct to the dance schools. It is also possible to raise funds through sponsorship and through charities, trusts and foundations. All these forms of funding are covered in more detail within the Drama section of this book, or check the Resources section.

Opportunity Knocks

THE FACE OF PERFORMING ARTS

For many years the performing arts did not reflect the rich racial mix of our society. This was truer in the drama and dance areas than in contemporary music where the influence of African, or more importantly, Afro-American culture was crucial to the development of jazz, the blues, soul music, and eventually hip hop and rap. Because of this there were many black musicians in the public eye, however there were very few black or Asian actors or dancers seen in our theatres, in films or on our TV screens – and if they did appear it was normally in a stereotypical role.

The situation over the past few years has changed quite rapidly, mainly because as society has become more racially integrated, more ethnic writers, directors, actors and dancers have brought their productions and performances to our stages and screens. Oscar wins for Denzel Washington and Halle Berry, starring roles for British actors such as Parminder Nagra in *Bend It Like Beckham* and *ER*, and Adrian Lester's magnificent performance as Henry V at the National Theatre and in the TV series *Hustle*, have increased our awareness of black and Asian actors. There are now many ethnic dance groups such as Adzido and Akademi. However, in January of 2004 an Iranian born actor, 33-year-old

Alan Marni, decided to sue his agency after being told he should forget about playing Shakespeare and go for roles as a terrorist or shopkeeper. Mr Marni is thought to be the first actor to sue his agency over discrimination.

SUPPORTING MINORITY GROUPS

Metier, the Sector Skills Council for the arts and entertainment industry, received £5 million of funding in 2001 to support the employment of minority ethnic people, people with disabilities and to challenge gender stereotyping, and although things are getting better, there are some areas that need improvement. People with disabilities are still under-represented in all areas of the performing arts, although the CandoCo contemporary dance company does run workshops for both able-bodied and disabled people (see Resources), and although many performers are of ethnic origin, it is still rare to see a black or Asian person backstage.

Meanwhile, the business and technical sides of the music scene are still dominated by men. Much of this is down to traditional perceptions of what men and women do – females in secretarial roles and men doing technical jobs (it's why they are known as 'the backroom boys') – and what areas of work people of ethnic origins have traditionally been employed in.

Tania Peach, the production manager at Mountview Academy is well aware of the problem:

'We only have one black student (on the technical side) here at Mountview and I am convinced it is to do with role models and that will not change until we, the people on the training side, start to change it. From the stage management and technical point of view there is nothing prohibitive at all, anyone can do this, whatever sex or race they are. Another way we can change things is through our community workshops where we can reach people who would not normally come into contact with the theatre or the dramatic arts.'

Below is the experience of one Asian actor in the theatre and on film and television over the past twenty years.

AMERJIT DEU, ACTOR

Amerjit's family is originally from India but he was raised in Leeds before attending the Douglas Webber Academy Of Dramatic Art in London. Over the last 20 years he has worked on stage, in TV (he played Dr Singh in *EastEnders*) and in films (he appeared in *Bend It Like Beckham*) and has seen attitudes to actors of ethnic origin slowly change.

'Although I have seen things change incredibly, I think discrimination is still there, but hidden. For example, when I did *EastEnders*, I remember asking the producers for various things that I knew the white actors on the set got, but I didn't. Asian actors still do tend to get typecast, but that applies more to older Asian actors than the younger actors. As an Asian you are still pigeonholed. Especially on British television we are seen as doctors, lawyers or cornershop owners! As an actor I do sometimes feel that casting directors should have more creative input because for a long time they have been scared. If it says in the script a young, middle-class couple in London, they tend to go for a white couple, while what they should say is "Ok, why don't we go for a black or Asian couple?"

'At the moment there are far more parts for young Asian and black actors. The TV show *Holby City* is fantastic as far as representing loads of ethnic backgrounds. There's a black nurse, a black surgeon, an Asian doctor and the patients are a total ethnic mix, just as it would be in a real hospital. However, *Coronation Street* hasn't really caught up with that yet, it is still very white.

'Shows like *Meet The Kumars* and *Goodness Gracious Me* have really helped our cause though because they have shown the majority of white, middle-class directors that Asian actors can play different roles, not just shopkeepers or accountants! I think the opportunities for young Asian and black people working in the performing arts are just going to get better and better. There will be more writers, directors and producers out there who come from multi-ethnic backgrounds and so it will make sense for them to be writing multi-ethnic parts and directing ethnic actors in those parts. There are more parts now for young Asian and black actors than there have ever been.'

The Final Word

Once you have finally trained and entered the real world of the performing arts you will very soon discover getting work is far from easy. If you have attended an accredited course that gives you automatic membership of either Equity or the Musicians' Union, then you will be at an advantage because prospective employers will consider you to be professionally minded. However, you will still have to audition and below are some pointers for getting that elusive job.

- Get yourself a professionally shot showreel or promotional photographs. These are not cheap but they may be a way of getting your foot in the door with casting directors.

- Get yourself an agent. Once again it will make you look professional and they may have access to audition information that you don't.

- Scour the industry publications and websites for news on jobs/shows/new companies being formed (see Resources for a comprehensive list).

- Be a good networker. Sometimes word of mouth can be the best way to find out about jobs.

- **Don't give up!** Performers have to take the psychological bumps when they are unsuccessful at auditions. Put it behind you and concentrate on the next job and the next audition.

- Take extra classes, learn new skills and concentrate on Continuing Professional Development (CPD). The performing arts don't stand still so nor should you.

- **Know your lines/notes/dance steps**. It cannot be emphasised enough that a professional attitude will get you work and keep you in work so practise and be prepared. This includes doing your homework on what the job is, who it is for, and how long it will last.

- **Smile.** Remember you are selling yourself, so smile, be personable, be interested and keep telling yourself that you are going to get that job – and you will!

The performing arts are currently thriving in Great Britain, mainly due to the fact we have more leisure time and disposable income than ever before and, being sociable by nature, we want to be entertained! That means going to the cinema, visiting the theatre, watching dance performances and listening to music. If you truly believe you have the considerable skills and talents it takes to make it in this extremely competitive world you will enjoy the added bonus of knowing you have a job doing what you love.

GOOD LUCK! Or should that be **BREAK A LEG!**

RESOURCES

FEATURED SCHOOLS AND COLLEGES

BRIGHTON INSTITUTE OF MODERN MUSIC (BIMM)
7 Rock Place
Brighton BN2 1PF
Website: www.bimm.co.uk

BRIT SCHOOL FOR THE PERFORMING ARTS AND TECHNOLOGY (BRIT)
60 The Crescent
Croydon CR0 2HN
Tel: 020 8665 5242
Website: www.brit.croydon.sch.uk

CANDOCO
CandoCo dance company provides workshops for both able-bodied and disabled people.
2T Leroy House
436 Essex Road
London N1 3QP
Tel: 020 7704 6845
Website: www.candoco.co.uk
Email: info@candoco.co.uk

MOUNTVIEW ACADEMY OF THEATRE ARTS
Mountview offers courses in acting, directing and technical theatre. It has an excellent reputation with masterclasses provided

by the likes of Lynn Redgrave and Mike Leigh. Former students include Amanda Holden.

Ralph Richardson Memorial Studios
Kingfisher Place
Clarendon Road
Wood Green
London N22 6XF
Tel: 020 8826 9216
Email: enquiries@mountview.ac.uk

NATIONAL FILM AND TELEVISION SCHOOL

Established in 1970 it is the most highly regarded film school in the country. The school functions as a postgraduate course so most students are slightly older than the average and many have already had some employment in the industry.

Beaconsfield Studios
Station Road
Beaconsfield
Buckinghamshire HP9 1LG
Tel: 01494 671234
Website: www.nftsfilm-tv.ac.uk
Email: admin@nftsfilm-tv.ac.uk

ROYAL ACADEMY OF DRAMATIC ART (RADA)

For many the Holy Grail of drama schools, its list of famous past members goes on endlessly (Sir Alan Bates, Ralph Fiennes, Jane Horrocks, Adrian Lester, Joely Richardson). Founded in 1904, it prides itself on its facilities, but mostly on the excellence of its training. As well as its full-time courses it offers short courses and, most importantly for the purposes of this book, a series of youth workshops during the year. These take place on a Saturday and are open to young people aged between 16 and 24. Refer to the website for details or send in a name and address to be included on the mailing list.

RADA
62–64 Gower Street
London WC1E 6ED
Tel: 020 7636 7076
Website: www.rada.org

ORGANISATIONS AND GOVERNING BODIES

BRITISH PHONOGRAPHIC INDUSTRY (BPI)
25 Savile Row
London W15 2ES
Tel: 020 7851 4000
Website: www.bpi.co.uk

BRITISH SOCIETY FOR MUSIC THERAPY (BSMT)
There is a reduced membership rate for full-time students who wish to become music therapists. Publishes the *BSMT Bulletin* and the *British Journal of Music Therapy.*

BSMT
61 Church Hill Road
East Barnet
Herts EN4 8SY
Tel: 020 8441 6226
Website: www.bsmt.org
Email: info@bsmt.org

CONFERENCE OF DRAMA SCHOOLS (CDS)
The Conference of Drama Schools (CDS) was founded in 1969 and aims to encourage the highest standards in training for the theatre, film and television industries. You can get further information on CDS member schools and the courses they offer in the 'CDS Official UK Guide to Drama Training'.

CDS
1 Stanley Avenue
Thorpe
Norwich NR7 0BE
Website: www.drama.ac.uk
Email: enquiries@cds.drama.ac.uk

COUNCIL FOR DANCE EDUCATION AND TRAINING (CDET)
The Council for Dance Education and Training has been set up to promote excellence in dance training provision in this country. It accredits courses at vocational dance schools and gives advice to schools, teachers, students and their parents. It also publishes a

wide variety of informative brochures answering the most often asked questions about becoming a dancer including 'An Applicant's Guide to Auditioning and Interviewing at Dance and Drama Schools' and 'A Practical Guide to Vocational Training in Dance and Drama Schools'. For information sheets, send an A4 stamped addressed envelope to:

CDET
Toynbee Hall
28 Commercial Street
London E1 6LS
Tel: 020 7247 4030
Website: www.cdet.org.uk
Email: info@cdet.org.uk

DANCE UK

This nationally recognised support agency has been set up by the profession to take action on its behalf. It has a wide range of useful information sheets aimed at professional dancers and dance students including 'Healthier Dancer Programme'. It also has a register of accredited medical and complementary practitioners to treat dancers.

Dance UK
Battersea Arts Centre
Lavender Hill
London SW11 5TF
Tel: 020 7228 4990
Website: www.danceuk.org
Email: info@danceuk.org

EQUITY

The British Actors' Equity Association is the trade union representing performers in arts and entertainment in this country. Its remit not only covers actors but also dancers, stage managers and even singers and directors. You can obtain a leaflet 'How to Join Equity' by writing to the address below, however if you are taking an accredited vocational course in the performing arts Equity offers a student membership, and for those who have completed such a course full Equity membership is automatically given.

Equity
Guild House
Upper St Martins Lane
London WC2H 9EG
Tel: 020 7379 6000
Website: www.equity.org.uk
Email: info@equity.co.org.uk

FOUNDATION FOR COMMUNITY DANCE

This national development agency provides information and support about employment and further training opportunities in fields as diverse as youth work, health, disability and the criminal justice system. It also publishes *Network News* fortnightly.

Cathedral Chambers
2 Peacock Lane
Leicester LE1 5PX
Tel: 0116 251 0516
Website: www.communitydance.org.uk
Email: info@communitydance.org.uk

INCORPORATED SOCIETY OF MUSICIANS

10 Stratford Place
London W1C 1AA
Tel: 020 7629 4413
Website: www.ism.org
Email: membership@ism.org

MUSICIANS' UNION

The Musician's Union has approximately 31,000 members and strongly defends those members' rights. It offers a variety of services including career advice and discounts on purchasing sheet music, instruments and equipment. It has 73 regional branches and covers six specialist musical areas: British Music Writers' Council, freelance orchestral, session musicians, folk, roots and traditional music, and jazz and theatre.

Musicians' Union
60/62 Clapham Road
London SW9 0JJ
Tel: 020 7582 5566

Website: www.musiciansunion.org.uk
Email: info@musiciansunion.org.uk

NATIONAL ASSOCIATION OF YOUTH THEATRES (NAYT)

The NAYT has a comprehensive list of amateur drama clubs and regional youth theatres it can send you.

NAYT
Darlington Arts Centre
Vane Terrace
Darlington DL3 7AX
Tel: 01325 363330
Website: www.nayt.org.uk
Email: nayt@aol.com

NATIONAL COUNCIL FOR DRAMA TRAINING (NCDT)

The NCDT was set up by the industry to ensure that drama training is of the highest quality and appropriate to the industry's ever changing needs. It provides general advice and information such as the funding available. You can obtain a list of NCDT accredited courses from the address below.

1–7 Woburn Walk
Bloomsbury
London WC1H 0JJ
Tel: 020 7387 3650
Website: www.ncdt.co.uk
Email: info@ncdt.co.uk

NATIONAL YOUTH THEATRE (NYT)

Scores of ex-members of the NYT have gone on to do great things within the industry. Anyone between 13 and 21 (or still attending full-time education) can apply and previous experience is valuable but not essential. Each year more than 3,000 young people are auditioned for NYT courses including Acting, Costume Making and Lighting and Sound.

NYT
443–445 Holloway Road
London N7 6LW
Auditions information line: 0845 903 9063
Website: www.nyt.org.uk

SOCIETY OF TEACHERS OF SPEECH AND DRAMA (STSD)

Behind every good actor is a good drama teacher – from Mrs Jones who taught them at 11 to the professionals giving them masterclasses at drama school. If you wish to become a drama teacher, the STSD can give advice and support.

STSD
73 Berry Hill Road
Mansfield NG18 4RU
Tel: 01623 627636
Website: www.stsd.org.uk

SPOTLIGHT

Founded in 1927, Spotlight now has over 30,000 members and provides casting information to the entertainment industry. For over 75 years its pictures and profiles of actors have helped casting agents pick the right person for the right job. It now has an award-winning Internet version of Spotlight with a comprehensive search engine for artist details. It also offers a dedicated video casting facility for its members.

Spotlight
7 Leicester Place
London WC2H 7BP
Tel: 020 7437 7631
Website: www.spotlightcd.com

PUBLICATIONS AND PERIODICALS

CONTACTS

The annual directory published by Spotlight and containing essential information for people working in stage, television, film and radio. Entries include a list of agents, dance companies and organisations, recording studios and theatre companies. Email info@spotlightcd.com or check the website at www.spotlightcd.com.

CRAC DEGREE COURSE GUIDES 2003/4: MUSIC, DRAMA AND DANCE

Published by Trotman, this gives comparative information on first-degree courses in the performing arts. The book covers the style and content of the courses, teaching and assessment methods and entrance requirements.

THE DIRECTORY OF GRANT MAKING TRUSTS

Published by Charities Aid Foundation, this lists all the places you can go to find funding for performing arts courses. Your local library should have a copy or contact:

CAF
Kingshill
West Malling
Kent ME19 4TA

UNIVERSITY SCHOLARSHIPS AND AWARDS

Author: Brian Heap. Published by Trotman, this lists scholarships available to students from universities and other organisations.

UCAS/TROTMAN PERFORMING ARTS COURSES 2005

This definitive guide published by Trotman gives an overview of courses in the performing arts offered in the UK, both at UCAS institutions and at privately run, accredited schools and colleges.

DANCE GAZETTE

Published three times a year by the Royal Academy of Dance, this has articles on dancers, dance companies, choreography, training and teaching.
Website: www.rad.org.uk
Email: gazette@rad.org.uk

DANCE NOW

This quarterly publication covers all aspects of theatrical dance and is aimed at both dance specialists and enthusiasts.
Website: www.dancebooks.co.uk
Email: now@dancebooks.co.uk

DANCE THEATRE JOURNAL

This quarterly magazine covers contemporary dance, ballet and non-western dance and includes interviews with choreographers and dancers.
Website: www.laban.org
Email: dtj@laban.org

DANCING TIMES

Aimed at performers and instructors, this monthly magazine mainly focuses on ballet and contemporary dance.
Website: www.dancing-times.co.uk
Email: dt@dancing-times.co.uk

MUSIC JOURNAL

The monthly magazine of the Incorporated Society Of Musicians (ISM). Covers news and activities and is read by professional musicians as well as music students.
Website: www.ism.org
Email: membership@ism.org

MUSIC TEACHER

A monthly magazine aimed at those involved in music education.
Website: www.rhinegold.co.uk
Email: music.teacher@rhinegold.co.uk

MUSIC WEEK

The music industry's weekly bible, covering everything from finances to new signings to legal news and distribution.
Website: www.musicweek.com
Email: martin@musicweek.com

OPERA

A monthly magazine covering opera events and music worldwide.
Website: www.opera.co.uk
Email: editor@operamag.clara.co.uk

OPERA NOW

This bimonthly magazine contains features, live reviews, interviews and profiles.
Website: www.rhinegold.co.uk
Email: opera.now@rhinegold.co.uk

SCREEN INTERNATIONAL

The movie industry's weekly bible. It has everything from news to statistics to film reviews.
Website: www.screendaily.com
Email: tim.dams@media.emap.com

SIGHT AND SOUND
A monthly magazine published by the British Film Institute (BFI)
and giving comment, news and features on films both old and new.
Website: www.bfi.org.uk
Email: s&s@bfi.org.uk

THE SINGER
A bimonthly magazine aimed at singers in all aspects of music
including classical, jazz, cabaret, choral and musicals.
Website: www.rhinegold.co.uk
Email: the.singer@rhinegold.co.uk

THE STAGE
The actors' weekly bible. It covers everything to do with the
entertainment industry including jobs, open audition dates and
new openings.
Website: www.thestage.co.uk
Email: listing@thestage.co.uk

VARIETY
This weekly newspaper is the American version of *The Stage* –
only with more glitz and glamour (as you'd expect as it gives the
inside gossip on Hollywood and Broadway). It also publishes
reviews of British theatrical shows and gives the top five charts of
movies, American TV shows and albums. Good to give you a taste
of what's actually out there.
Website: www.variety.com
Email: adam.dawtrey@reedbusiness.com

GOVERNMENT AND AWARDING BODIES

CONNEXIONS
Connexions is aimed primarily at 13- to 19-year-olds and gives
excellent information on jobs and careers. The Connexions Card
enables students to earn 'points' as they study. In the Career Zone
section of the Connexions Card website the Career Bank can offer
you detailed information on getting into dance, drama and music
as well as having links to related careers in the entertainment
and leisure sector including stage manager, drama therapist and
arts administrator.

Website: www.connexions.org.uk or
www.connexionscard.com

DEPARTMENT FOR EDUCATION AND SKILLS (DfES)
If you are undertaking a vocational training course lasting up to
two years (with up to one year's practical work experience if it is
part of the course), you may be eligible for a Career Development
Loan. These are available for full-time, part-time and distance
learning courses and applicants can be employed, self-employed
or unemployed. The DfES pays interest on the loan for the length
of the course and up to one month afterwards. You can also
obtain information on funding for state funded Higher Education
courses and on Dance and Drama Awards (DaDAs). The DfES also
has a list of Centres of Vocational Excellence in the performing
arts around the country.

Packs available from 0800 585505
Website: www.dfes.gov.uk
or www.dfes.gov.uk/cove

EDEXCEL
Edexcel is now responsible for BTEC qualifications including
BTEC First Diplomas, National Diplomas and Higher Nationals
(HNC and HND). The website includes qualification quick links.
BTEC qualifications in this field include Technical, Performance,
Production, Makeup, Musical Theatre, Set Construction, Stage
Design, and Circus Skills as well Acting, Dance, and Music.
There have been recent changes to Edexcel so please check the
website carefully.

Stuart House
32 Russell Square
London WC1B 5DN
Tel: 0870 240 9800
Website: www.edexcel.org.uk

LEARNDIRECT
This free helpline and website can give you impartial information
about learning.
Tel: 0800 100 900
Website: www.learndirect.co.uk

LEARNING AND SKILLS COUNCIL
Launched in 2001, Learning and Skills Council (LSC) now has 48 branches across the country and is responsible for the largest investment in post-16 education and training in England.
Modern Apprenticeship Helpline: 0800 150600
Website: www.lsc.gov.uk or
www.realworkrealpay.co.uk (specifically aimed at those who would like to do Modern Apprenticeships (MAs))

FOR MAs IN SCOTLAND YOU SHOULD LOOK AT
Website: www.modernapprenticeships.com or
www.careers.scotland.org.uk

FOR MAs IN WALES YOU SHOULD LOOK AT
www.beskilled.net

METIER
Metier is the sector training organisation specifically for the arts and entertainment sector. It has an excellent database of consultants and training providers and if you need advice on funding or on the careers available in this sector you should check out the website. It also publishes the *Arts Training Journal*.

Metier
Glyde House
Glydegate
Bradford BD5 0BQ
Tel: 01274 738800
Website: www.metier.org.uk
Email: admin@metier.org.uk

SKILLSET
Skillset is the industry organisation set up to look after training for the independent and freelance sectors of the film, television, video, and radio industries. It collects information on existing training provision and promotes adequate training for new entrants.

Skillset
124 Horseferry Road

122 PERFORMING ARTS UN

London SW1P 2TX
Tel: 020 7306 8585
Website: www.skillset.org
Email: info@skillset.org

WITHDRAWN

Books are to be returned on or before
the last date below.

For enquiries or renewal at
Ardleigh Green LRC
Tel: 01708 455011 Ext: 2040